PR
Collected
Middle English
Literature

8/04

Medieval Lyrics of Europe

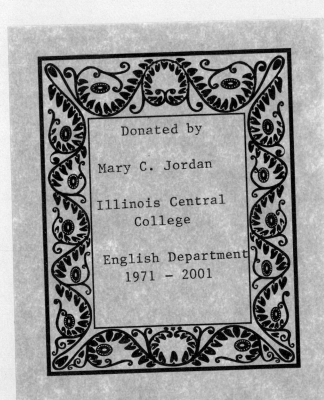

Medieval Lyrics of Europe

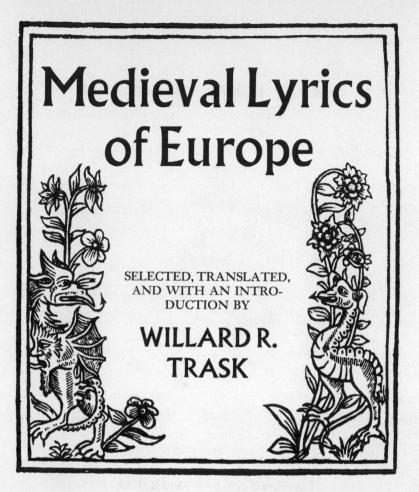

Medieval Lyrics of Europe

SELECTED, TRANSLATED,
AND WITH AN INTRO-
DUCTION BY

WILLARD R. TRASK

AN **NAL** BOOK

THE WORLD PUBLISHING COMPANY

NEW YORK AND CLEVELAND

FOR *ALEXANDER GODE VON AESCH*

First printing—March, 1969

Published by The New American Library, Inc.
in association with The World Publishing Company
2231 West 110th Street, Cleveland, Ohio 44102

Manufactured at World Publishing Press, a division
of The World Publishing Company, Cleveland, Ohio.

Library of Congress Catalog Card Number: 68–23848

PRINTED IN THE UNITED STATES OF AMERICA

CONTENTS

II · FRENCH

III · GERMAN

IV · ITALIAN

V · MOZARABIC

VI · SPANISH

INTRODUCTION

I

THE EARLIEST RECORDS of lyric poetry in the Middle Ages have come down to us in the form of condemnations. Early in the sixth century Bishop Caesarius, of Arles in Provence, complained of "country people, men and women, knowing by heart and singing diabolical love songs." A hundred years later the ecclesiastical Council of Châlons, held in northern France, anathematized dancing to "obscene and filthy songs." In 847 Pope Leo IV forbade women to sing and dance in churches and churchyards. Some light on the nature and performance of such songs comes from Iceland in the twelfth century: "There was a play men used much, which was unseemly, wherein a man would recite to a woman in the dance effeminate and satirical poems, and a woman to a man love verses." About the year 1124 one Luce de la Barre had his eyes put out for making and singing songs against Henry I of England.

Apart from two largely unintelligible lines of Provençal[1] preserved in a Latin poem of the tenth century, the earliest surviving fragments of European medieval lyric that have come down to us are in Mozarabic (the variant of Spanish then spoken in Andalusia), preserved as quotations in poems of a certain type by Arabic and Hebrew poets. Arabic histories of poetry name Muqaddam of Cabra, of the ninth century, as the originator of the *muwashshah*, as this type of poem was called. But none of his work has been preserved; the earliest Mozarabic song fragment that can be certainly dated occurs in a *muwashshah* composed in A.D. 1042. In all, some fifty of these Mozarabic *kharjas* (as they are named from the function they serve in the Arabic and Hebrew

---

[1] The term "Provençal" has lately been called into question, since the geographical boundaries of the language did not coincide with those of the province. But it is consecrated by usage, and a better has not yet been suggested. "Provence," as here used, has the same extended application.

poems) have so far been recovered, the last of them dating from the late thirteenth century.[2]

The composers of the Mozarabic fragments are unknown. The first Romance poet both whose name and some of whose lyrics have come down to us is Guilhem de Peitieu (as he is known in the Provençal in which he composed; or, in French, Guillaume de Poitiers), seventh count of Poitiers and ninth duke of Aquitaine (1071–1127). He succeeded to his father at the age of fifteen; he is said to have composed and recited a poem, now lost, on his adventures in the First Crusade, from which he returned in 1102; so that his poetical activity may be considered to have begun by the last decade of the eleventh century.

That Guillaume's poems were preserved is doubtless due to the fact that he was one of the most powerful princes of his time; the domains that he inherited from his father were far more extensive than those of the King of France. We know, for example, of a contemporary of his—Eble, viscount of Ventadorn—who was also a poet, but none of whose poems has come down to us. But Guillaume's rank and influence sufficed to set a fashion. From the next Provençal generation, poems not only by noblemen but by mere wandering minstrels were recorded and preserved.

And in fact the fashion for lyric poetry spread not only through Provence itself, but northward to France and Austria and southward to Italy, Portugal, and Spain.

In France the earliest known lyric poet is Chrestien de Troyes (flourished 1160–1180). That the fashion of which he is the first French representative came from Provence may be read in the fact that his patroness, Marie de Champagne, was a granddaughter of Guillaume de Poitiers.

Whether the earliest lyric poets composing in the German language, Kürenberg and Dietmar von Eist (both Austrians), were or were not influenced by Provençal poetry is still a much debated question. In any case, their immediate successor, Meinloh von Sevelingen (flourished 1180) shows

---

[2] They were not discovered until 1948. Work on their recovery and interpretation is still going forward.

some Provençal influence; his successors, in their turn, accepted it wholeheartedly.[3]

Dante not only gave a place in his *Comedy* to Bertran de Born, Arnaut Daniel, and Sordello (who, though an Italian, composed in Provençal), but cited Arnaut, with other Provençal poets, as examples of the highest art in his essay on vernacular poetry. Yet in acknowledging their mastery he was but following the lead of the earliest Italian lyric poets, who themselves were the most nearly Provençal of all the schools influenced by Provence. Firm dates for individual early Italian poets are particularly hard to come by. However, we know that the earliest group—the "Sicilians," as they are called, though not all of them were from Sicily—flourished at the court of the Hohenstaufen emperor Frederick II, who was born in Sicily in 1194 and made Palermo his principal capital until his death in 1250. Frederick was a poet himself; but it seems more likely that some one of the other "Sicilians" was the first of the school. The Provençal poet Raimbaud de Vaqueiras (ca. 1155–1207) composed a dialogue between himself and a woman of Genoa, in which he speaks in Provençal and she in Italian; and Sordello of Mantua and Bonifacio Calvo of Genoa (both thirteenth century) composed their lyrics in Provençal.

In all these countries, not only the ideas and attitudes of Provençal poetry but also the most complex of its forms had found acceptance. In Spain and Portugal, though its ideas and attitudes crossed the borders, its forms fell by the wayside. The earliest extant Portuguese lyric, by King Sancho I, was probably composed in 1189. It shows no sign of the Provençal influence which was to become abundantly apparent in the next generation of poets. Yet, significantly enough, here again a man of high rank suddenly turns up doing what none of his forebears are known to have done—composing poetry, even as had Guillaume de Poitiers.

---

[3] As is the case with "Provençal," the linguistic and geographical boundaries of "German" do not coincide. The medieval lyric in German appeared first in Austria, whence it spread to Germany proper; it was also cultivated in Switzerland, the Netherlands, Belgium, and Bohemia. To indicate this fact, the names of their countries of origin are given with the names of the "German" poets in Section III.

The author of the earliest extant Spanish lyric (first half of the thirteenth century; it is actually narrative in form, but lyric in atmosphere) tells his audience that he studied in Germany, France, and Lombardy. Like many a later student, he seems to have loved France best, for his poem is almost purely French, both in meter and manner. After him, there is a curious situation: except for a few lyric interludes in narrative poems in Castilian Spanish, when Spanish poets composed lyrics they did it in the language of Galicia (which at that time was almost indistinguishable from Portuguese) and in the forms developed there and in Portugal. Spanish lyric poetry in Castilian does not begin until the fourteenth century. By that time Provençal poetry was dead in Provence (killed there by the horror of the Albigensian Crusade). But its stock of ideas and attitudes had already reached the Peninsula directly, and they were now reimported into Spain by way of Italy.[4]

II

From this account it would appear that the medieval lyrics of these various languages must have a strong family likeness. And so they do. But it is a likeness, not an identity. Far from any two of them being twins, they are not even full sisters. They are more like half-sisters with the same father but with different mothers.

It is here that the usual surveys of medieval lyric—at least down to the arrival of such individual poets as Dante and Villon—tend to falsify the picture. This is due to an almost exclusive concentration on the full-dress love lyric in which the man of the couple is the speaker—the canzon (Provençal, *canso, canson*), together with its most direct descendant, the Italian *canzone*. The picture presented is that of an extremely complicated technique put entirely at the service of an almost hieratic attitude. As poet, the composer is first of all concerned to invent for each new poem a stanza whose pattern of longer and shorter lines and whose rhyme scheme have never been used before. As lover, his only concern is

[4] I am preparing a study and anthology of medieval Galician-Portuguese poetry, with translations. The reader is referred to this forthcoming volume for examples not included here.

to present himself and his lady (who, for good measure, is always a married woman) in the one approved posture—she scornful, unattainable, a creature of a higher world; he hopeless yet devoted, a mortal whom her cruelty has doomed to a lingering death which, because it proceeds from her, he reckons as joy.

As far as it goes, it is a true picture. All these elements of the lover's attitude are already present, at least germinally, even in the lyrics of Guillaume de Poitiers. Certain elements of a more earthy sensuality which are also found in Guillaume's work and in that of the earliest generation of Provençal poets were soon dropped, and the whole conception was refined to the almost excruciating purity of Dante's immediate predecessors.

But even within the Provençal *canso* itself, there are things which give this stilted picture the lie.

Among the composers of Provençal lyrics, the names of a dozen women have come down to us and, among their extant works, a dozen love poems. We also have a few anonymous poems in which the speakers are women, and two of the same type composed by known men poets.[5]

To read these is to enter a different world. Here it is the lady who pleads, the man who is disdainful. So far, it might seem to be the same old scene, only with the woman speaking the lines of the man. But no; for the lover is not only disdainful, he has been what he could never possibly be in *his* canzons, he has been unfaithful. And what does the lady want? She wants him back. And back to what? Back in the bed they have shared—her bed, where now she dreams of him, only to wake and find that he is not beside her. It would be hard to imagine a situation more different from that of the lover and his lady in the men's love songs.

[5] This last practice was not uncommon in medieval poetry. Some of the poems were composed by men for women who could not compose their own; others seem to have had no occasion but the poet's wish to try his hand at something different. Villon composed a prayer to the Virgin at the request of his illiterate mother. It is interesting that, in modern times, Padraic Pearse, president of the first ill-fated Irish republic, did the same thing for *his* mother while he was in prison awaiting execution.

III

Then too, the love song, whether man's or woman's, does not exhaust the repertory of the canzon. The form was also used for elegies, not only on dead ladies but also on dead princes; for satire, on subjects from woman's dress through rival poets to the church and war; for poems occasioned, in one way or another, by the Crusades; for hymns to the Virgin and exhortations to righteousness; for argument; for humor. All these, in their several ways, are a far cry from the image drawn from no other evidence than the classic man's love song.

In each of these many kinds, the canzon shows the same preoccupation with form which, as we have seen, attended the composition of the man's love song. It is here that its greatest accomplishment lies. The structural experiments of generations of Provençal poets, leading eventually to the Italian *canzone* and the sonnet, hammered out forms which have remained viable in Western poetry down to yesterday and even today. Structurally considered, Keat's "Odes" are still Provençal poems. After a long lapse into prettiness, the sonnet is rejuvenated in the work of Gerard Manley Hopkins and E. E. Cummings.

IV

But if the canzon accounts for the greater number of Provençal poems it is not the only form in which they were composed. Beside it, we have a small but precious collection of poems with stanzas less complex and with refrains. Outstanding among these is the group of *albas* (dawn songs), so called from the fact that the word *alba* (dawn) always appears in the refrain. Here, again, we are in another world from that of the man's love song: the two lovers are in bed together, and the poem itself is their lament that dawn has come to end their lovemaking.[6]

Of the same world, too, is the handful of dance songs (*dansa, balada*) that has come down to us in Provençal.

---

[6] Poems of this type occur in a great many literatures, including those of peoples—some of them primitive—who are entirely outside the Western literary tradition. The significance of this fact for its bearing on "origins" can scarcely be overemphasized.

But the dance songs also have another importance. Though few in Provençal, in northern France and Italy they are counted in hundreds; the great majority of even the men's love songs in Portuguese and Spanish are in short stanzas with refrains; and, though they were not much cultivated in their original form in Austria and Germany, a whole school of German-speaking poets delighted in adapting the content of the dance songs to the exigencies of the canzon form.

Are we to suppose that the dance song was, like the canzon, imposed from Provence? All other considerations aside, the differences in form between the dance songs of the various countries make this most improbable.

In addition, we have the testimony of the Mozarabic *kharjas*. These, as we saw, are pre-Provençal. The majority of them are women's songs. And though the evidence as we have it does not suffice for proof, some of them probably did not exist alone, but were themselves the refrains of dance songs. Women's dances, be it remembered, were the particular object of the ecclesiastical condemnations (also pre-Provençal) quoted at the beginning of this introduction.

It looks, then, very much as if the dance songs descend, not from Provençal, but from indigenous lyric poetries of the various countries. I, at any rate, believe that this is so. If it is, it lends an extraordinary interest to these songs, which, charming as they are, have often been held to be of only slight importance. If it is, it accounts for the fact that the various medieval European lyric poetries are not sisters but only half-sisters. If the father was always Provençal, the mothers were, in each case, the indigenous variety of dance song.[7]

V

Two points with a more particular bearing on the individual poems in this collection must be mentioned, and indeed emphasized.

First: With the exception of the early Italian examples,

[7] This Introduction is not the place even to review the lengthy controversy over the origins of medieval European lyric poetry, since the question cannot be dealt with on the basis of translations alone.

all medieval lyrics before about 1300 were *songs*. At first the poet himself composed both melody (*son*) and text (*vers*). Later he became content to have his words set by a professional musician or wrote them for a preexisting tune. To stress the fact that these poems were meant to be sung, I have referred to them as "songs" in the titles which I have given them. (With the rarest exceptions, medieval lyrics have no titles of their own.) I have also added, as an appendix, a discography of those poems in this anthology whose music has been preserved and recorded.[8] I hope that the reader may listen to some of these, and then try to imagine the other poems as delivered in the same way.

Second: There is no such thing as an agreed text of a medieval lyric. To say nothing of variations in individual words, even the order of stanzas differs in different manuscripts. There are also frequent passages in which the work of generations of editors has not succeeded in clearing away the errors of the scribes who copied the manuscripts. In such cases I have, as a translator, done what, as an editor, I should be debarred from doing: I have supplied a meaning resting not on the unintelligible text but on the intelligible context. The references to sources are only meant to direct the interested reader to a more or less accessible publication of some version or versions of the original.

V I

It is the variety, rather than the classic monotony, of medieval lyric poetry that I have sought to present in this anthology. Though the hieratic man's love song is—as it must be—present, the hitherto comparatively neglected woman's song is given due place beside it. All the other genres of the canzon enumerated above are also represented.[9] And there is a plentiful representation of dance songs and of songs in forms derived from the dance. The Index of Types, ap-

[8] Unfortunately, only a very small proportion of the melodies of medieval secular songs has been preserved. In Provençal, for example, we have the words of some 2600 songs, but only some 240 melodies.

[9] Except the argumentative. Stripped of the technical brilliance of rhymes and stanza forms, the argumentative poems make a dull showing.

pended to the Introduction, will serve both to exhibit this variety and to make it possible for the reader to compare examples of any particular genre in the various languages.

The choice of poems in a given anthology must necessarily reflect a combination, in various proportions, of traditional acclaim and personal preference. It would be impossible, for example, to omit from a medieval anthology such a long-praised poem as Jaufre Rudel's song to his lady far away.[10] I have tried to give an adequate representation of these, or at least of such of them as did not seem, despite my best efforts, to lose all their value in a mere prose translation. However, a "major poet" is often "major" almost as much by reason of the bulk of his work as by anything else; so that one particular poem by a "minor poet" may well be better, or in some way more attractive, than any one particular poem of the "major's." This consideration, together with my wish to give adequate representation to women's poems, anonymous poems, and dance songs, has led me to select a good many poems which have never before been translated into English.

I have been a devotee of medieval poetry now for some thirty years. The renewed and intensive frequentation of it necessitated by selecting and translating the poems here presented has left me only admiring and enjoying it the more. I hope that the reader of this anthology will derive from it something of the pleasure that I have had in producing it.

W. R. T.

Juniata College,
Huntingdon, Pennsylvania
Spring, 1968

[10] Its fame dates from the Middle Ages themselves; it is preserved, in one form or another, by sixteen manuscripts (in one of them as a translation of the Provençal original into French). And at least since Rostand made it the subject of his play *La Princesse Lointaine*, it has become *the* medieval lyric, as Jaufre himself has become *the* medieval lyric poet.

INDEX OF TYPES*

* References are to pages.

I · PROVENÇAL

Guilhem de Peitieu, Duke of Aquitaine
(1071 — 1127)

[1] LOVE SONG *Ab la doussor del temps novel*

With the sweetness of the new season the woods leaf and birds sing, each in its own language, following the measure of a new song; this is indeed the time when it is good for a man to have what he most desires.

But from there where, for me, are all that is best and most beautiful, neither messenger nor letter comes. So my heart knows neither sleep nor laughter, I dare not take a step until I learn for certain that the end will be as I would have it.

It is with our love as with the hawthorn branch that shakes on the tree all night under the rain and frost, until day comes and the sun shines out on green leaf and branch.

I still remember one morning when we made peace, and she gave me the greatest of gifts: her love and her ring. May God let me live until the day when I have my hands under her cloak!

I care nothing for this strange talk which would separate me from my Good-Companion, for I know how it is with words and these hints that go round. Someone or other is always boasting of love. But we—we have the loaf and the knife!

Good-Companion: poetical name for the poet's lady.

Cercamon
(fl. 1137 — 1152)

[2] LOVE SONG *Quant l'aura doussa s'amarzis*

When the sweet breeze turns bitter and the leaf falls from the branch and the birds change their language, I, too, sigh here, singing of love that holds me a prisoner in bonds, for never yet have I gained mastery over it.

Alas! I have won from love only its torments and its toil; nothing is harder to attain than what a man most wants, nothing is so desirable as what a man cannot have.

Yet one joy I have to make me glad: she whom I love more than ever I loved anything. When I am with her I am so confounded that I cannot tell her my longing, and when I leave her I feel as if I had lost my mind and all that I ever knew.

Compared with her, I would not give so much as a glove for the most beautiful and accomplished woman the world has ever seen. When the whole of creation grows dark, where she is it is light. May God spare my life until I possess her or can see her go to bed.

I neither live nor die nor get better nor even know how sick I am, though I am very sick. For I am no diviner, to know how much of her love I shall have or when, for in her is all the grace that can lift me up or cast me down.

Awake or asleep, I shiver and quake and tremble for love of her. I so fear she will abandon me that I cannot think how to ask her for what I want. Well, I will serve her for two years or three, and then perhaps I shall know the truth of it.

If she will not have me I wish that I had died on the day she accepted me into her service. God! how sweetly she killed me when she showed me signs of love! For she has killed me, and yet—I know not why—there is no other woman I want to see.

I rejoice when she drives me mad or keeps me on tenter-hooks or stupidly gaping; I am glad when she makes sport of me or twists me around her finger. For after all this evil, good will quickly come to me if she so pleases.

It depends on her whether I am false or true, upright or deceitful, base or the flower of courtesy, awkward or at ease.

Cercamon says: There is little courtesy in a man who despairs of love.

Alas! whomever it pleases or displeases, I am hers to keep if she wants me.

Jaufre Rudel, Prince of Blaye

(fl. 1140)

[3] ON HIS LADY FAR AWAY *Lanquan li jorn son lonc en mai*

In May when days are long I take delight in the sweet singing of birds far away; then, when I am gone from there, I remember a far-away love. And my heart is so dark and bowed down that neither songs of birds nor hawthorn blossoms delight me any more than freezing winter.

Never shall I taste love's joy if I enjoy not that far-away love, for I know no more beautiful or better lady anywhere, either near or far away. Her worth is so true and perfect that, there in the Kingdom of the Saracens, I would gladly be made a prisoner for her sake.

I shall think it great joy when I beg her, for the love of God, to give lodging to a stranger from far away, and, if she pleases, I shall lodge close to her, though now I am far away. That will be the time of high talk, when her lover from afar will be close enough to enjoy her presence and her fair words.

Sad and happy will I go from her if ever I see that far-away love; but I know not if ever I shall see her, our countries are apart so far—many ways and roads lie between and I am no prophet. But let it all be as God wills!

I believe that he is true to his word, the true Lord through whom I shall see my far-away love. Yet for one good that comes to me from her I receive two evils, for she is so far away. Oh that I were a pilgrim there, for my staff and cloak to be seen by her lovely eyes!

God, who made all that comes and goes and made this far-away love, give me the power—for I have the will—soon to see my far-away love, present with me in such places that, bedroom or garden, I shall think a palace forever!

He speaks truth who says that I am filled with desire for a far-away love. For no other joy so delights me as enjoying a far-away love. But what I would have is denied me. For my godfather put a charm on me that I should love and not be loved.

But what I would have is denied me. May he be damned forever, the godfather who put a charm on me that I should not be loved!

Marcabru

(fl. 1150)

[4] HE TALKS WITH A CRUSADER'S LADY *A la fontana del vergier*

By the spring in the orchard where the grass grows green down to the gravel I found, sitting all alone under a fruit tree, among the pleasant white flowers and the pleasant new singing of birds, her who will not make me happy.

She was a young girl beautiful of body, daughter of the lord of a castle. And as I was thinking that the birds and the green leaves and the sweet new season were bringing her joy so that she would listen to what I had to say, suddenly her mood changed.

There by the fountain she wept, and sighed from the bottom of her heart. "Jesus," she said, "King of the world, it is you who cause my great grief, it is the shame put upon you that undoes me, for the best men in all this world are going to serve you—but such is your will.

"My lover is going to you, he who is handsome and courteous and brave and noble; here with me remains distress, and often longing and tears. Oh, a curse on King Louis, who gives the orders and commands the preaching that have made grief enter my heart!"

When I heard her lamenting I went to her by the clear stream. "My beauty," I said, "too much crying spoils a girl's face and complexion. And you have no reason to despair; for he who makes the woods come into leaf can give you joy in full measure."

"Sir," said she, "I truly believe that God will have mercy on me in the other world, and on many more sinners. But here he takes from me the one thing that brought me a growing joy—but little did it last, for my lover has gone too far away."

King Louis: Louis VII of France, who organized the Second Crusade.

Bernart de Ventadorn

(fl. 1150 — after 1170)

[5] TO HIS LADY, ON THE JOY OF LOVE *Pel doutz chan que·l rossinhols fai*

At the sweet song that the nightingale sings in the dark when I am asleep I wake in a daze of joy, thinking deeply of love. And I can do nothing better, for always I welcome joy, and with joy my song begins.

If joy were to be seen or heard anyone knowing the joy I feel would find all other joy little compared with mine, my joy is so great. Many a man struts and boasts, thinking that he is running over with true love—when I have twice as much as he!

When I see her happy body, so well made that no one could ask more, when I see her courtesy and hear her fair speech, my power to praise fails me; I should need a whole year to tell the truth of her, so courteous is she and so exquisite.

They who believe that I am present here do not know that my spirit is close to her where she is, even though my body is far away. I tell you: the best messenger I have from her is my own thoughts, which bring her beauty back to me.

Lady, yours I am and shall be ever, ready to do your bidding. I am your sworn liegeman and long have been. You are my first joy, and you shall be my last while life is granted me.

I do not know when I shall see you again, but I go from you now in grief and despair. Because of you I have parted from the king, and I ask you not to let it turn to harm for me. For among ladies and knights at every court I will be ready to serve you in all loyalty and sweetness and humility.

Little Hugh, my courteous messenger, be so good as to sing my song to the Queen of the Normans.

the king: Henry II of England.   *the Queen of the Normans:* Eleanor of Aquitaine, wife of Henry II.

[6] ON LOVE AND SONG AND HIS LADY *Non es meravelha s'eu chan*

It is no wonder if I sing better than any other singer, for my heart draws me more to love and I am better fitted for love's rule. Body and heart and mind and thought and strength and all that I can, I have given to it. The bridle so turns me to love that I heed nothing else.

Truly he is dead in whose heart there is no savor of love. And what use is it to live in such baseness—except to disgust people? May the Lord God never hate me so much as to make me live on for a month, a day, if ever I earn that disgust or have no more desire to love!

In loyalty and truth I love the most beautiful and best of women. My heart sighs, my eyes shed tears, for I love her so much that I suffer by it. But what else can I do, if love takes me prisoner and no key except pity can open the dungeon in which he has put me, and I find no pity there?

How gently this love pierces my heart with its sweet savor! A hundred times in a day I die for grief, and live again for joy a hundred more. Truly, my evil is a fair thing, too, being better to have than another's good. And since my evil is thus good, good indeed will be the good that will come after such torment.

Would to God that true lovers could be seen for what they are among the false lovers and that backbiters and betrayers had horns on their foreheads! I would gladly have given all the gold in the world and all the silver, if I had them, only for my lady to know how truly I love her.

When I see her anyone can tell it from my eyes, my face, my color; and I shake with fear like a leaf in the wind. I have not sense enough for a child, so does love hold me. On a man thus conquered, a lady may well have mercy.

My good lady, I ask nothing of you but that you take me to be your servant; for I will serve you as a good suzerain, let my reward be what it may. See, I am yours to command, O noble, gracious, bright, courteous one; you are no bear or lion to kill me if I yield to you.

For My-Courteous, I send this poem to the place where she is, and may she not be angry that I have been so long away from there.

My-Courteous: poetical name for the poet's lady.

Bertran de Born

(ca. 1140 – before 1215)

[7] PRAISE AND ADMONITION *Be·m platz lo gais temps de pascor*

I like the gay spring season that brings out leaves and flowers. I like hearing the birds rejoice, making the woods ring with their songs. I like seeing tents and pavilions set up in the fields. And my joy is great when I see knights and horses deployed in line on the plain.

I like it when the scouts set people running with their possessions. And I like seeing a great host of armed men crowding after them. I enjoy it with all my heart when I see strong castles besieged and their outworks broken and ruined and see the host on the bank protected on all sides with palisades of strong stakes set close together.

I like it, too, when a lord fearlessly leads the attack on his armored horse, for so he fills his men with daring courage; and after the battle is engaged each must be ready and willing to follow him, for no man is worth a button until he has given and taken many a stroke.

Maces and swords, painted helmets and shields—as soon as the battle begins we shall see them hew and shatter, as many vassals strike together, and then the horses of the dead and wounded will run wild. Once in the thick of the fight every man of birth must think of nothing but smashing heads and arms, for better it is to be dead than to live defeated.

I tell you, the pleasures of eating and drinking and sleeping are nothing to me compared with hearing both sides shouting "At them!" and unmounted horses whinnying in the shade and cries of "Help! help!" and seeing lords and common men alike falling on the grass by the ditches and the dead with their sides pierced by broken lances still bearing pennons.

Barons one and all, pawn your castles and cities and towns rather than stop fighting!

Countess of Dia
(probably fl. 1160)

[8] LOVE SONG *Estat ai en greu consirier*

I have been in bitter torment for a knight who was mine, and I would have it known for all time how more than much I loved him. Now I see that I am betrayed because I did not give myself to him in love, and great sorrow I have had for it night and day.

Would that I could hold my knight once after dark in my bare arms, and that he would be happy with me for his pillow! For I take more delight in him than ever Floris did in Blanchaflor; I give him my heart and my love, my mind, my eyes, and my life.

Fair lover, full of grace and goodness, when shall I have you in my power? When, in bed with you one night, can I give you a kiss of love? Believe me, I should be greatly glad to have you in place of my husband, on only one condition: that you had promised me to do all that I would have you do.

Floris ... Blanchaflor: hero and heroine of a romance of which an Old French version has been preserved.

[9] LOVE SONG *A chantar m'er de so qu'eu no volria*

I must sing of what I would not, such cause have I to complain of my lover, for I love him more than anything in the world. Yet nothing avails me with him—neither pity nor courtesy, nor my beauty nor my worth nor my intelligence, for I am as much deceived and betrayed as if I were a slut.

For consolation I have the thought that I have never been guilty of any fault toward you, my lover; indeed, I love you more than ever Seguis did Valensa, and I am glad that I outstrip you in love, for in all else, my lover, you are the better. But you are haughty toward me in word and look, though toward all others you are free and open.

I am amazed that you can be so haughty toward me, my lover, and I have reason to complain of it. For it is not right that another love should take you from me, no matter what she says to you or allows you. Remember the beginning of our love. God forbid that our separation should be my fault!

Your very qualities and your fair fame make me uneasy, for I know of no woman near or far who, if she is ready to love, would not be drawn to you. But you, my lover, with your intelligence, should be able to tell which is the truest in love. Remember the promises we exchanged.

My worth and my birth should speak for me, and my beauty, and, even more, my true heart. So I send this song to you in the place where you are, to be my messenger. And I would know, my fair and noble lover, why you are so fierce and cruel to me—I do not know if it is pride or ill will.

But most of all I would have my messenger tell you this: Too much pride has brought many to great harm and grief.

Seguis . . . Valensa: hero and heroine of a lost romance.

Giraut de Bornelh
(fl. 1165 — 1199)

[10] DAWN SONG IN DIALOGUE *Reis glorios, verais lums e clartatz*

The watcher:

"Glorious King, true light and brightness, God, omnipotent Lord, if it be thy pleasure give loyal help to my friend, for I have not seen him since night fell—*and soon it will be dawn!*

"Fair friend, do you sleep or wake? Sleep no more, rise and make no sound. For in the east I see the star brightening that brings the day, I know it well—*and soon it will be dawn!*

"Fair friend, I summon you with my song. Sleep no more, for I hear the birds singing as they search the woods for day. I fear the jealous one will catch you—*and soon it will be dawn!*

"Fair friend, come to the window and look at the signs in the sky; you will see if I am a true messenger. If you do not, you will suffer for it. *And soon it will be dawn!*

"Fair friend, since I parted from you I have neither slept nor risen from my knees, praying to God, son of blessed Mary, that he would give you back to me in loyal friendship. *And soon it will be dawn!*

"Fair friend, there on the steps you begged me not to grow drowsy, but to keep watch all night until day; but now you like neither my song nor my company. *And soon it will be dawn!*"

The lover:

"Fair, gentle friend, I am in so precious a place that I wish neither dawn nor day would ever be again. For in my arms I have the loveliest woman ever born; holding her, little I care for dawn or for the jealous fool!"

the jealous fool: the lady's husband.

Raimbaut de Vaqueiras

(ca. 1155 — 1207)

[11] GIRL'S SONG [L]*Altas undas que venez suz la mar*

Great waves coming over the sea, with the wind tossing you this way and that, can you tell me news of my lover, who has crossed the water? I do not see him come back. *Oh, God of Love, now he gives me joy, now grief!*

Sweet breeze that comes blowing from where my lover sleeps and lives and lies, bring me a drink of his sweet breath. I open my mouth in longing for it. *Oh, God of Love, now he gives me joy, now grief!*

It is a bad thing to love a man from another country, for all his play and his laughter turn to tears. I never thought my lover would fail me, for I gave him all that his love asked of me. *Oh, God of Love, now he gives me joy, now grief!*

would fail me: The text reads *me tenys*, which makes no sense here. Anglade renders: "would behave in this way (?)." Some such meaning was obviously intended.

The Monk of Montaudon

(fl. 1180 — 1210)

[12] PRAISE *Mout mi platz deportz e gajeza*

I like pleasure and gaiety, and hospitality and liberality and splendor, and an openhearted, well-mannered lady quick at answering. I like affability in a nobleman and severity in him toward his enemy.

I like a man who speaks to me pleasantly, and a man who is ungrudging in giving to me, and a nobleman who does not dress me down. I like hearing good news, and sleeping when it blows and thunders, and a fat salmon for lunch.

I like it well in summertime to be by a fountain or stream when the fields are green and the flowers revive and the birds sing sweet and my mistress comes and I do it to her, once, quickly.

And I like a man who receives me graciously and does not fob me off with false promises. I like being gay with my mistress and kissing her and the rest if it comes to that. And if my enemy is set back, I like it—and the more so if I do it myself.

And I like friends when I am among my enemies, so that I can speak up for my cause and they will hear me out.

Peire Bremon lo Tort

(fl. 1200)

[13] SONG SENT TO HIS LADY FROM SYRIA
*En Abril, quan vei verdejar**

In April, when I see the green fields greening and the orchards flower and the streams run clear and I hear the small birds sing, the scent of the flowers and the grass and the sweet song that the bird cries out make my joy live again.

In that season I used to think how I could gain the gladness of love—with riding and display, with serving and honoring; for he who is master of those arts makes love glad, and so the easier to win.

I sing who should weep, for the grief of love keeps me in languishment. I think perhaps I can cheer myself by singing. But I never heard of a man who sang when he should weep. Even so, I do not despair; I shall yet have reason to sing.

No, I must not despair wholly because I cannot yet see my lady. For God who made me forsake her has the power to bring me back to her. And if once I am where she holds sway, if ever I go back to Syria may God never let me come home again!

God must have been amazed that he could never part me from her, and have been much pleased with me when I consented to leave her for him. For he knows that if I lost her I should never feel joy again nor could he give me anything to take her place.

Well she knew how to steal my heart when I took leave of her to come here; for not a day passes that I do not sigh, remembering the fair thing that was in her face. For she said to me, all woebegone: "What will become of me who love you, my lover? Why are you leaving me?"

Song, make your way across the sea and go, in God's name, to my lady and tell her that I am in pain and grief for her night and day. And, good song, tell Guillelm the Far-sighted that I ask him to sing you to her and to go and comfort her.

* Probably composed in 1197.

Gui d'Ussel

(fl. 1200)

[14] PASTORAL *L'autrier cavalcava*

The other day I was out riding in bright fair weather, when I saw a shepherdess whose face had the freshness of youth. She was singing prettily; then she stopped where the song said: "Evil is life to one who has lost joy."

Quickly I turned my reins toward where she was singing. She got up graciously and came hurrying to meet me. At such openhearted kindness and such beauty I dismounted at once, to show fit courtesy to her who received me so charmingly.

"Well-mannered girl," I said, "please do not be afraid to tell me what that song was you were singing just now when I came here. For never, I assure you, did I hear any shepherdess sing so well."

"Sir, not long ago I had at my bidding him who now causes me sorrow because I have him no longer, he forgets me for another woman; that is why I complain and why, too, I sing to forget the grief that is killing me."

"Girl, I will tell you frankly that I, too, have been wounded, just as you have by him who forgets you—in my case by a woman of no decency whom I loved very much. Now she wrongfully forgets me for another—would that he were dead!"

"Sir, you shall find reparation for the wrong that frail-hearted woman has so foully done you. Here I am, at your service, for I love you and shall for the rest of my life if you are willing. So let us turn the sorrows we have both suffered into joy and gladness."

"Charming, openhearted creature, you will fulfill my every desire if you are willing; you bring my ship to joyful port, delivered from all perils."

"Sir, your love has perfectly freed me and cured me. I have forgotten my wrong. Your sweetness has ended all my misery."

Dame Tibors

(fl. 1220 — 1245)

[15] LOVE SONG *Bels dous amics, ben vos puosc en ver dir*

Fair, sweet friend, I can tell you in all truth that never have I been without desire since you have been with me as my true lover, never have I been without a longing, fair, sweet friend, to see you as often as might be, never have I repented of loving you, and never, if you left me in anger, have I known joy until you came to me again.

Bertran d'Alamano
(fl. 1230 – 1260)

or Gaucelm Faidit
(fl. 1180 – 1215)

[16] DAWN SONG *Us cavaliers si jazia*

A knight was lying beside her whom most he wanted; kissing her again and again, he said: "Sweet, what shall I do? For day is coming and night is going. *Oh, I hear the watchman calling, 'Up and away! I see day on the heels of dawn!'*

"Sweet, could there be neither dawn nor day ever again, it would be a great blessing, at least wherever a true lover was with his best delight. *Oh, I hear the watchman calling, 'Up and away! I see day on the heels of dawn!'*

"Sweet, whatever anyone tells you, never believe that there is pain like that which parts lover and beloved; I know it from what I feel now. Alas! how little of night there is! *Oh, I hear the watchman calling, 'Up and away! I see day on the heels of dawn!'*

"Sweet, I must go. Wherever I am, I am yours. In God's name do not forget me. For the heart of me stays here, and will never leave you. *Oh, I hear the watchman calling, 'Up and away! I see day on the heels of dawn!'*

"Sweet, if I were not to see you, I should be dead before long, believe me; my great desire would kill me. So I shall soon return; for without you I have no life. *Oh, I hear the watchman calling, 'Up and away! I see day on the heels of dawn!' "*

Peire Cardenal

(fl. 1220 — 1270)

[17] LEAVE-TAKING *Be teing per fol e per muzart*

I say the man is a fool and wasting his time who becomes entangled with love. For in love he comes off worst who has most trust; one who thinks he is only warming himself finds that he is burned. The good of love is slow in coming, the evils come every day. Fools, criminals, and frauds—it is these who make up love's company. For my part, I am done with it.

My mistress shall never keep me hers unless I keep her mine, nor enjoy me unless I enjoy her. I have taken good counsel and shall follow it: I will do to her as she does to me. If she deceives me she will find me a deceiver; if she goes straight with me I will go straight.

I never gained so much as when I lost my mistress. For, losing her, I gained myself that I thought I had lost. Little does he gain who loses himself. But he who loses what harms him I hold is the gainer. For I had given myself, I swear, to one who was destroying me, I know not why.

So giving, I put myself, my heart, and my life at her mercy who is fickle and forsakes me and changes me for another. He who gives more than he keeps or loves another more than himself chooses misery, for he neither looks out nor stands up for himself. He forgets himself, and no good comes to him for it.

I now take leave of her forever, not to be hers again. For never did I find faith or decency in her, but crookedness and falsehood. There are sweets full of poison. For love blinds a man's eyes and turns him from his path when he loves what he should not love and suspects and abandons what he should love.

To a faithful mistress a man should be faithful. But her who puts her trust in deceit, it is right that he should deceive as much as he can. So it pleases me when, as sometimes happens, such a woman runs foul of a man who deceives her, guarding his honor from harm and himself from folly, nor lets the bit turn him.

Cerveri de Girona
(fl. 1250 — 1280)

[18] VIADEYRA (Song for the Road) *Nol prenatz los*
fals marit

> *Never take him, your false husband,*
> *Lovely Jana!*
>
> Never take him, your false suitor;
> He is a fool and knows nothing,
> *Lovely Jana!*
>
> Never take him, your false husband;
> He is a fool and half asleep,
> *Lovely Jana!*
>
> He is a fool and knows nothing;
> Never love him,
> *Lovely Jana!*
>
> He is a fool and half asleep;
> Never let him go to bed with you,
> *Lovely Jana!*
>
> Never love him;
> The man you have in secret is better,
> *Lovely Jana!*
>
> Never let him go to bed with you;
> Your lover will do better for you there,
> *Lovely Jana!*

Guiraut Riquier
(fl. 1252 — 1294)

[19] SONG TO THE VIRGIN *Yeu cujava soven d'amor chantar**

Often in times past I thought that I was singing of love; yet I knew it not, for what I called love was my folly. But now love brings me to love such a lady that I can neither honor her nor fear her nor cherish her to the measure of her worth. But I hope that her love will hold me until the hope that I have in her is fulfilled.

For by her love I hope to increase in worth and honor and riches and joy. To nothing else, then, should I turn my thought or my desire. For, since all that I want I can have through her, I must do all that I can to serve her. For I have her love, if only I behave toward her as true love teaches me to do.

And so I must try my best: since she loves me, let me, too, love, for I could not love her if she did not give me the power. Hence it is only right that, for her love, I should give mine. For without her I am good for nothing. I can do nothing for her except to honor her. God, who has the power, grant that I may hold before my lady the banner of true lovers among whom love reigns.

I have neither wit nor knowledge to praise her; such is her honor that there is room for no more, such her virtue that nothing can increase it. How, then, can my praise honor her? The honor is mine, for I can only speak what is true. Hence I must do my best to tell the truth of her from morning to evening; for I can never fail in anything that I should do, if only I remember my lady.

So great is her beauty that it can never lessen, there is no imperfection in it, it shines night and day. So great is her power that it cannot fail. Such are her kindness and charity and wisdom and knowledge and pity and mercy that I hope her love—since she deigns to love me—will keep me joyful, if only I truly come to her.

Fittingly can I name my lady My-Fair-Joy, for I have good hope that she will make me such a man as it is right that I should be; wherefore I beg her, of her grace, to restore me.

I am not jealous, whoever may seek the love of her whom I love. Indeed, I rejoice in it, and take great offense at such as will not love her. For I truly believe that through her love all good comes.

I beg my lady to succor her lovers so that each of them may attain his desire.

* Composed in 1289.

Anonymous Canzon and Stanzas

[20] WOMAN'S SONG *Quan vei les praz verdesir*

When I see the fields grow green and the flower come into bud, I think long of love that has so taken me; a little more, and it would kill me. Often I sigh, for never did I hear of such a blow without a stroke being struck. *Aei!*

All night I sigh and lie awake, or start in my sleep because I seem to feel my lover waking. Oh God, I should be cured of all this if one night—what good fortune!—he came to me. *Aei!*

A lady whom love holds must have high courage. There are men who will take her now, then leave her for a whim. But my heart is true to him, so loyally that never was lady of my birth so loyal. *Aei!*

Let any lady who has no lover beware and never take one; for love stabs today and tomorrow, and so fiercely that there is no moment of relief from it. Without a blow, it kills and wounds; she cannot be cured, not by any doctor in the world, unless love brings remedy. *Aei!*

Messenger, rise early, for you have a long journey to make. You must carry this song to my lover in his country. Tell him that I am very happy if he remembers the song that he sang to me after he kissed me under my bed-canopy. *Aei!*

Into my curtained room he came like a thief. There in my curtained room he was my prisoner.

[21] WISH *Gran deszir ay de ben iaszer*

A great desire have I to be well bedded—on a featherbed of love, with the beautiful girl who has me in her power making me a coverlet over her; the bolster should be her golden hair and the sheet joy and laughter and the pillow her white arms and the mattress orchard or meadow!

[22] A DREAM *Un cavaler conosc qe l'altrer vi*

I know a knight who, the other day, met a most beautiful and charming lady; and he was delighted when, putting back her cloak, he saw her body and her face and her hair. And that night when he went to sleep he dreamed of her. Shall I tell you how he put an end to his dream? With another lady, who was there beside him.

[23] RIPOSTE *Ma domna am de bona guiza*

I love my lady well enough but not so much as to make a fool of myself over her; gladly would I have her undying love but not if I have to spend money to get it. May God never save me or help me if ever I do anything for her that she would not do for me. I think that, if I give her my love, I honor her as much as she does me.

Anonymous Dance Songs

[24] DANCE SONG *A l'entrade del tens clar*

When the bright season comes in—*eya!*—
The Queen, to bring back joy again—*eya!*—
And to vex the jealous one—*eya!*—
Has a mind to show how she is given to love.
Away, away, jealous one, leave us, leave us
to dance by ourselves, by ourselves!

She has sent word everywhere—*eya!*—
That from here even to the sea—*eya!*—
Not a girl or a lad—*eya!*—
Shall fail to come and dance in the joyous dance!
Away, away, jealous one, leave us, leave us
to dance by ourselves, by ourselves!

But here comes the King—*eya!*—
To stop the dance—*eya!*—
For he is in dread—*eya!*—
That someone will carry off his April Queen.
Away, away, jealous one, leave us, leave us
to dance by ourselves, by ourselves!

But he is wasting his pains—*eya!*—
For what cares she for an old man?—*eya!*—
She wants a gay lad—*eya!*—
Who knows how to give her pleasure, the delectable lady!
Away, away, jealous one, leave us, leave us
to dance by ourselves, by ourselves!

Oh, whoever sees her dancing—*eya!*—
Moving her lovely body—*eya!*—
Would say in all truth—*eya!*—
"She has not her match in the world, the Joyous Queen!"
Away, away, jealous one, leave us, leave us
to dance by ourselves, by ourselves!

[25] DANCE SONG *Coindeta sui, si cum n'ai greu cossire*

Pretty I am, but I am wretched,
All on account of my husband, for I neither
love him nor want him.

And I will tell you why I am so desirous:
—*Pretty I am, but I am wretched*—
Because I am young, a girl just grown,
—*Pretty I am, but I am wretched*—
And I ought to have a husband who would make me happy,
And with whom I could play and laugh all the time.
Pretty I am, but I am wretched,
All on account of my husband, for I neither
love him nor want him.

May God never save me if I love him,
—*Pretty I am, but I am wretched*—
I do not even want to love him,
—*Pretty I am, but I am wretched*—
Truly, when I see him I feel so ashamed of him
That I pray to death to come and kill him soon.
Pretty I am, but I am wretched,
All on account of my husband, for I neither
love him nor want him.

But I have made up my mind to one thing:
—*Pretty I am, but I am wretched*—
If my lover loves me better than ever,
—*Pretty I am, but I am wretched*—
There lies the good hope to which I hold!
I weep and sigh because I do not see him.
Pretty I am, but I am wretched,
All on account of my husband, for I neither
love him nor want him.

And I tell you what I have made up my mind to:
—*Pretty I am, but I am wretched*—
Since my lover has loved me so long,
—*Pretty I am, but I am wretched*—
Now I will give him all my love
And the good hope that I love and want so much.
Pretty I am, but I am wretched,
All on account of my husband, for I neither
    love him nor want him.

To this tune I make a pretty dance song
—*Pretty I am, but I am wretched*—
And pray that people will sing it everywhere
—*Pretty I am, but I am wretched*—
And that every right-thinking lady will sing it,
About my lover whom I so much love and want.
Pretty I am, but I am wretched,
All on account of my husband, for I neither
    love him nor want him.

[26] DANCE SONG *Quant lo gilos er fora, bel ami*

When the jealous one is away, fair friend,
Come to me!

I am making a gay pretty dance song,
—*When the jealous one is away*—
Whether anyone likes it or not,
—*When the jealous one is away*—
To the sweet tune that quiets me
For I heard you singing it night and morning.
When the jealous one is away, fair friend,
Come to me!

My lover, if I had you
—*When the jealous one is away*—
In my own fine bedroom,
—*When the jealous one is away*—
I would kiss you for joy,
For I heard good words of you the other day.
When the jealous one is away, fair friend,
Come to me!

If the jealous one threatens me
—When the jealous one is away—
With a stick or a club,
—When the jealous one is away—
Even if he comes to beat me,
My heart will not change!
When the jealous one is away, fair friend,
Come to me!

II·FRENCH

Chrestien de Troyes

(fl. 1160 — 1180)

[1] LOVE SONG *D'amors qui m'a tolu a moi*

Of love, which has taken me from myself yet will not make me of its company, I complain even as I surrender to its will. Yet complain I must, and for this reason: those who betray love I often see attaining its joy, while I have failed of mine through my steadfast loyalty.

If love, to glorify its creed, tries to convert its enemies, it is only right, I think, that it should not fail its true followers. For my part, who cannot renounce her to whom I bow, I send her my heart, which is hers; yet I count it no service, for I am but paying her what I owe her.

Tell me, lady, are you grateful to me for being your servant? Not at all, if I know you at all! Indeed, you find it a burden to have me. And since you do not want me I am yours for your displeasure. But if ever you are to show pity to anyone, bear with me—for I can serve no one else.

I never drank the brew that poisoned Tristan; but my true heart and my steadfast will make me love more than ever he did. Greatly should I be thanked for it, for nothing forced me to it except believing my own eyes. It was that which set me on the path that I shall never leave and have never tired in.

Heart, if my lady is ungracious to you do not forsake her for that; still be ruled by her, unchanging in what you have begun. Never, I say, can you love enough; let not bad times dismay you. Waiting for a thing sweetens it; the more you have longed for it, the sweeter it will be when you taste it.

I should find pity where I seek it, I know, if there were such a thing in the world; but I fear there is not. Tirelessly I pray to my lady. Though I profit nothing by it I implore her again and again, being one who can neither deceive nor make a game of love.

Richard I, Cœur de Lion

(1157 – 1199)

[2] SONG FROM PRISON *Ja nus hons pris ne dira sa reson*

No man held prisoner will ever truly speak his mind without complaining. But to cheer himself he can make a song. I have many friends, yet little do they give. It will be shame to them if, because of my ransom, I am held prisoner these two winters.

Well do my men and my barons know—Englishmen, Normans, Poitevins, Gascons—that not the meanest of my followers would I leave in prison for money's sake. I say it not in reproach—but I am still held prisoner.

Now I know it for truth that a dead man or a prisoner has neither friend nor family, seeing myself abandoned for gold and silver. I am concerned for myself, but much more for my people: when I am dead they will suffer great blame, so long am I held prisoner.

It is no wonder my heart grieves when my liege lord is ravaging my lands. If now he remembers the oath that we swore together, I know well that I should not long be held prisoner here.

The young men of Anjou and Touraine—rich now in wealth and health—know well that I am held far from them in a stranger's hands. They loved me greatly, now they love me not at all. Fields of arms lie bare, stripped of gallant deeds because I am held prisoner.

To my comrades whom I loved and love, they of Cahors and they of La Perche, say for me, song, that they are faithless, for I was never false to them or weak in their cause. They do most shamefully if they make war on me now, when I am held prisoner.

Le Chastelain de Coucy

(died 1203)

[3] LOVE SONG *Coment que longe demore*

Though I long ago left off singing I have good reason to sing again. For love has made me forget the long anguish that was killing me, and has given me new hope. Lady, for whom I gladly sing, have mercy!

Believe me, lady, one who is courteous despite offense is honored for it. Nor have I ever heard a good word spoken for one who, having the advantage, shows cruelty. Since the love I bear makes me love you more than myself, God grant it may remind you that a gentle heart should show mercy.

Love, you have put me in deadly peril, for it is your doing that she to whom you have given me cares nothing for me. I am dying by your whim. But it will be a shame to you, I say, if you do not make my dying so sadden her that she will show me mercy.

Mercy is so darkly hidden from me that I cannot see it. Much as I long to know it and feel it, I believe that, for me, pity and beauty are divorced. It must be so, lady, since in you I have found no mercy.

It is a great sin—and great labor besides—to feign love-service, as these false, empty men do who pretend without feeling. Then why does God grant them the power to lie so glibly? While I, who would rather die than do as they do, know only one word as I have only one desire: Mercy!

Love, you are no better than a churl if you begin your work only to drop it. For a love that must be renounced is worse than death. You could practice no greater treachery against one whom you hold in your power. You make him a king— and then nothing. Lady, I put myself in your hands. Have mercy!

Richart de Semilli

(late 12th century)

[4] DANCE SONG *J'aim la plus sade riens qui soit de mere nee*

I love the most winning creature that was ever born;
All my heart and body and mind are set on her.
Good God! what can I do with this love that is killing me?
A woman who would love should be modest in the street,
But in a room with her lover let her laugh and play and give
herself!

No one could help loving her, her grace is a wonder,
She is whiter than a flower, red as a rose.
Good God! what can I do with this love that is killing me?
A woman who would love should be modest in the street,
But in a room with her lover let her laugh and play and give
herself!

She has pale blonde hair, gray eyes, a winsome mouth,
A body made to be held, her bosom is white.
Good God! what can I do with this love that is killing me?
A woman who would love should be modest in the street,
But in a room with her lover let her laugh and play and give
herself!

She has a small foot and it is well shod,
And how gracefully she walks in the street!
Good God! what can I do with this love that is killing me?
A woman who would love should be modest in the street,
But in a room with her lover let her laugh and play and give
herself!

What more can I say? No other woman can match her.
If only she would take pity on me she would be perfect.
Good God! what can I do with this love that is killing me?
A woman who would love should be modest in the street,
But in a room with her lover let her laugh and play and give
herself!

Song, go to her quickly, you will find her gentle and sweet;
Tell her to sing you over and over. Oh, how well she sings!
Good God! what can I do with this love that is killing me?
A woman who would love should be modest in the street,
But in a room with her lover let her laugh and play and give
herself!

Gace Brulé

(fl. ca. 1180 — 1210)

[5] LOVE SONG *Cil qui d'amours me conseille*

He who advises me to turn from love knows not what it is
that keeps me sleepless nor how grievously I sigh. He who
reproves me and never loved in his life is stupid, for no one
but a fool meddles in things of which he knows nothing.

Ha! white, bright, rosy one, all my desires turn to you; you
are such a miracle that reason and right fall short. No right
could grant you to me as a mistress. If your great courtesy,
garnished with all goodness, does not deign to help me it
was an evil day for me when first I heard you so highly
praised.

It is a poor heart that becomes discouraged and is ready to
die of fear. The stout heart arms itself with good hope of
better things. But nothing that I say, lady, can avail me, for
I ask too much. If a breath of baseness, delighting in treachery, makes you renounce pity I saw you for my ruin, I cry
for death.

He who goes gaping after what is too high may well hear
much that he will not like. But all that great love deigns to
take in keeping, it makes equal; love's most high power
raises and lowers. Sweet lady, help! She who rules me can
well guide and lift up my presumptuous desire.

In my heart a climbing vine is ready to flower: true love,
courteous and faithful, if there were one to fulfill it. But love
that is not fulfilled cannot make a joyful heart. Well I see
it, my lady and my enemy: unless death chastens my desire I cannot be less presumptuous nor renounce the beauty
of my offending.

Conon de Béthune

(died 1217)

[6] ON JOINING THE CRUSADE *Ahi! Amours, con dure departie*

Alas, O Love, a hard leave-taking this that lies before me from the best woman that man ever loved or served! May God in his mercy bring me back to her as surely as I grieve to part from her. Wretch, what have I said! Never do I part from her. If my body goes to serve Our Lord, my heart remains in her keeping.

Sighing for her, I journey to Syria, for I must not fail my Creator. Let all know that whoever fails him in this need, he will fail in a greater. Let great and small alike know, too, that the place to do knightly deeds is where paradise is to be won and honor and fame and praise and a lady's love.

Good God! we have boasted so much of courage; now it will be seen who is truly brave if we go to avenge the painful shame at which every one of us should feel ashamed and angry, for in our time the holy place is lost where God suffered agony and death for us; if now we leave our mortal enemies there, our life will be a shame to us forever.

Let him who would not drag out a wretched life here go there to die for God in happiness and joy, for that death is sweet and savory by which we gain the rich kingdom. No, not one will go down to death, they shall be born into the life of glory. And whoever comes back alive shall be greatly happy; honor shall be his bride forever.

All churchmen and men of years who persevere in almsgiving and good works—they shall share in this pilgrimage, and ladies who live chastely and remain loyal to those who go. Women who listen to evil counsel and follow lewdness will practice it with cowards and wicked men, for all good men will be gone on this journey.

God is besieged in his holy kingdom: now will it be seen how they come to his aid whom he freed from dark prison when he died on the cross that now the Turks hold. Be sure of this: they who will not go are utterly dishonored, unless they are poor or old or sick, and those who are healthy and young and rich cannot remain behind without shame.

Alas! I go weeping my eyes out there where God wills to make my heart better. And you may well believe that I shall be thinking more of the best woman in the world than of the journey.

[7] SATIRE *L'autrier avint en cel autre pais*

Not long ago, but a long way from here, there was a knight who loved a lady. As long as the lady was in her prime she rejected and refused his love. But a time came when she said to him: "My friend, I have put you off with words many a day. By now your love has been tested and proved. Henceforth I am yours to command."

The knight looked at her and saw that her face was pale and faded. "Lady," he said, "it is too bad that you would not let me know your feeling years ago. Your face that was as beautiful as a lily has so gone from bad to worse that there seems to be nothing left of you for me."

Shamed by such scorn and mockery, the lady tried to brazen it out with lies. "By God, fellow," she answered, "I was only making a fool of you. Did you think I really meant what I said? By God, it never even crossed my mind to sink to loving you. What you like best is kissing and hugging some handsome page boy!"

"By God, lady, I have certainly heard talk of your beauty, but it is all gone. I have heard tell of Troy, too, that once it was a most noble city, and now even the site of it is lost. So I advise you, lady, to stop trying to make a heretic out of anyone who chooses not to love you from now on."

"By God, fellow, you will live to regret having brought my age against me. Even if I had worn out all my youth I am rich and of the noblest blood; men would love me without caring if I had beauty or not. Why, not two months ago, the Marquis sent me a messenger, and De la Barre jousted for love of me."

"By God, lady, this way you have of forever thinking about high birth has done you great harm. A man does not love a lady for her rank. He loves her when she is spirited and intelligent. Time will show you that this is the truth. A hundred men have wept for love of you who will never take you now—not if you were daughter to the King of Carthage!"

Guiot de Dijon

(fl. ca. 1220)

[8] SONG FOR A CRUSADER'S LADY *Chanterai por mon corage*

I shall sing, trying to cheer my heart, lest I die or go mad from the great hurt that I feel, seeing no one come back from that cruel land where he is who soothes my grief when I hear talk of him. *God! when they cry "Forward still," help the pilgrim, Lord, for whom I am in fear, for dread are the Saracens!*

I shall suffer what now I suffer until I see him come back. He is on pilgrimage. Much I long for his return, for despite my kindred I will not marry anyone else—they are wasting their breath who talk of it. *God! when they cry "Forward still," help the pilgrim, Lord, for whom I am in fear, for dread are the Saracens!*

This is my heart's grief—that he is not here on whom I have set my will. I have neither play nor laughter by him now. Yet he is handsome and I am beautiful. Why, O Lord, have you done this? When we desire each other, why do you part us? *God! when they cry "Forward still," help the pilgrim, Lord, for whom I am in fear, for dread are the Saracens!*

This is my pure happiness—that he pledged himself to me. When the sweet air blows from the most sweet country where he is for whom I long, gladly I turn my face to it. God! I seem to feel him under my gray cloak. *God! when they cry "Forward still," help the pilgrim, Lord, for whom I am in fear, for dread are the Saracens!*

This is my great regret—that I could not see him off. Instead, he sent me a shirt he had worn, for me to embrace. At night when love of him torments me I take it into bed with me, close against my naked flesh, to soothe my grief. *God! when they cry "Forward still," help the pilgrim, Lord, for whom I am in fear, for dread are the Saracens!*

Colin Muset
(fl. 1234?)

[9] A MINSTREL THINKS OF WINTER *Quant je voi yver retorner*

Winter is coming in: I wish I could settle down. If only I could find a generous host, no pinchpenny, with a store of pork and beef and mutton, wild duck, pheasants and venison, fat fowl and capons, and good cheeses in straw!

And the lady of the house should be as liberal as her husband, ready to please me night and day as long as I stayed, and the host should never be jealous of her but often leave us alone together. Oh, then I should have no wish to ride, mud-splattered from head to foot, after a worthless bad-tempered prince!

Duchess of Lorraine

(13th century)

[10] ELEGY *Per maintes fois aurai estei requise*

Often I have been asked why I do not sing as I used to. But I am so far from joy that I would do a better thing: would that I could die even as she did whose example I would follow, Dido slain for love of Aeneas.

Fair, sweet lover, why did I not do all that you asked of me while I had you? The churls whom I feared so hurt and hindered me that I could never reward you for your service. If that were possible, I would repent of it even more than Adam repented for the apple that he took.

By God! love has brought me to great grief. Churl Death, who wars on all mankind, you have taken from me what I most loved. Now I am the Phoenix, alas! alone and bereft, the single bird of which they tell. Now I will grieve, who once rejoiced. Sorrow and travail shall be all my portion.

Never did Anfelise do as much for Foucon as I would do for you, my love, if I had you back again; but, for that to be, I must die . . . Would that I could change, but love has dominion over me.

Anfelise . . . Foucon: legendary heroine and hero.

Richart de Fournival

(fl. 1265)

[11] GIRL'S SONG *Onques n'amai tant que jou fui amee*

I did not love as much as I was loved. Now I am sorry for it—not that being sorry is any use. For love had destined me to the best and handsomest man in all this countryside, from whom I should have had all joy and honor; but now he has given his love to another, one who has taken him to her eagerly. Woe to the day that ever my mother bore me! My pride has lost me my lover.

May God never grant me a lasting love if I did not love him dearly and purely when he told me that he loved me; but I dared not tell him the truth of it, fearing the talk of slanderers. Fair Lord God! would that he had kissed me and embraced me and lain with me then; if he had given me his love, the whole world was welcome to look on!

Now love has destined me to evil, making another possess what I love and never letting me stop thinking of him nor ever have joy or comfort by him. Alas! the love that I refused him so sternly I offer him and give him wholly now. But I have spoken late, for I have lost him. Now I must love and not be loved, for I have conquered my hard, wicked heart too late.

Adam de la Halle
(died 1288)

[12] RONDEAU: LOVE SONG *Tant con je vivrai*

So long as I live I shall love none other than you. Never will
I leave you so long as I live. No: I will serve you faithfully,
to whose service I have given all my being. So long as I live
I shall love none other than you.

Philippe de Remi
(fl. 1270 — 1285)

NONSENSE VERSES

[13] *Uns grans harens saurs*

A big red herring was besieging Gisors from both sides and
two dead men came to reinforce it, carrying a door. If it
had not been for an old tart shouting "get out" at them, the
cry of a dead quail would have tried to catch them under a
felt hat.

[14] *Li pes d'un sueron*

A cheese mite's wind hit a lion so hard that it went through
him. The pith of a reed took hold of a lump of mud, which
flew into a rage and called "Stop, thief!" Suddenly the beak
of a fledgling bird drove them so far apart that a gosling's
feather carried off Paris.

Guillaume de Machaut

(ca. 1300 — 1377)

[15] BALLADE: ALLEGORY *De toutes flours n'avoit et de tous fruis*

Of all flowers and fruits I had none in my garden except one rose. The rest had been stripped and killed by Fortune, who now presses hard on that sweet flower to destroy its color and scent. But if I see it picked or laid low I will never want another after it.

Yet I cannot imagine that the virtue which clothes it could come from you, Fortune, with your crooked ways. No, that is the gift of its own nature. So I venture that you will never be strong enough to take away its beauty and its worth. Leave it for me, then; for neither in my garden nor elsewhere will I ever want another after it.

Ha! Fortune, pit gaping to swallow whoever is so foolhardy as to believe your false teaching! I find no good nor truth in it, but only deceit. Your laughter, your joy, your honor are tears and sorrow and disgrace. If your false tricks blight my rose, I will never want another after it.

[16] RONDEAU: LOVE SONG *Rose, lis, printemps, verdure*

Rose, lily, spring, green leaves, flowers, balm, sweetest scent —lady, you are more sweet than these, and more beautiful.

In you are all gifts of Nature to make me adore you: rose, lily, spring, green leaves, flowers, balm, sweetest scent.

And since your worth surpasses all created things, well may I say in all truth: Rose, lily, spring, green leaves, flowers, balm, sweetest scent—lady, you are more sweet than these, and more beautiful.

Jean Froissart
(?1333 — ?1400)

[17] VIRELAI: FOR A LADY *Par un tout seul escondire*

By just one "Get you gone" that my lips spoke but not my heart, I drove my lover away, and now the pain of it will kill me.

Alas for what my lips did! How dared they speak the very opposite of what my heart desires? Sadly I weep and sigh. Yet I have done nothing wrong. I only drew from my lips the sword that kills me.

By just one "Get you gone" that my lips spoke but not my heart, I drove my lover away, and now the pain of it will kill me.

If ever he comes back to me, may God punish me if I do not very soon return to where love draws me. I mean to content my heart no matter what my lips may do. Let them scream and shout if they choose, my heart will not quail.

Eustache Deschamps
(?1346 — ?1406)

[18] VIRELAI: GIRL'S SONG *Sui je, sui je, sui je belle*

Am I, am I, am I beautiful?

It seems to me—or so I think—that I have a good forehead and a sweet face and pretty, red lips. *Tell me if I am beautiful.*

I have eyes that change color, narrow eyebrows, blonde hair, a straight nose, a round chin, a slim white throat. *Am I, am I, am I beautiful?*

I have firm, high-placed breasts, long arms, slim fingers, and narrow hips. *Tell me if I am beautiful.*

I have good loins—or so I think—a good back and good buttocks such as you find in Paris, and well-shaped legs and thighs. *Am I, am I, am I beautiful?*

I have small, high-arched feet, and well shod too, and pretty clothes; I am gay and merry. *Tell me if I am beautiful.*

I have cloaks lined with fur, I have hats, I have plenty of money and lots of silver pins. *Am I, am I, am I beautiful?*

I have plain silks and watered silks, I have cloth of gold, and white cloth and gray; I have many pretty things. *Tell me if I am beautiful.*

I am not fifteen yet, and so I tell you. My treasure is a very pretty thing, and well I will keep the key to it! *Am I, am I, am I beautiful?*

He will have to be bold who becomes my lover, who wins such a girl. *Tell me if I am beautiful.*

And I promise and swear I will be faithful to him as long as I live, if he does not falter. *Am I, am I, am I beautiful?*

If he is courteous and kind, but hardy withal, and mannerly, he will win his cause. *Tell me if I am beautiful.*

It is paradise on earth to have a lady who is always so fresh and new. *Am I, am I, am I beautiful?*

As for you who are afraid to try, you had better think about what I say. Here ends my song.

Am I, am I, am I beautiful?

Christine de Pisan
(1365 — 1431?)

[19] ON THE DEATH OF HER HUSBAND *He!*
Dieux, quel dueil, quel rage, quel meschief

O God, what grief, what fury, what ruin, what defeat, what sad and evil fortune for me, alas! who suffer such torment as no living creature ever endured! I curse the destiny that draws out my life. For I have but one desire: to die. I have no heart to go on living, he being dead who kept me alive.

O cruel Death, you put an end to all my good days—what cruelty!—when you took him from me who was all my good and my protection; whereby you have brought me so low, I swear, that I wish my grieving, weary, darkened soul were torn from my body, he being dead who kept me alive.

And if my weary, grievous days were short, at least the grief I endure would end. But that is not to be. No—I shall live on in mourning without end or measure, in tears and lamenting, in bitter longing. I look for nothing but to suffer these assaults. It is only right that I should so wear out my days, he being dead who kept me alive.

Charles d'Orléans
(1394 — 1465)

[20] SONG FOR A LADY *Mon seul amy, mon bien, ma joye*

My only love, my good, my joy, whom I love above all other men, I beg you to be joyful, expecting that I shall see you soon.

For I do nothing but look for a way to come to you; so help me God! my only love, my good, my joy, whom I love above all other men.

And if wishing could bring me together with you even for a day or two, not for everything under heaven would I wish for anything else, my only love, my good, my joy.

[21] LOVE SONG *Le voulez vous*

Will you have it so, shall I be yours? Captured or rescued, I yield myself your prisoner.

One word for many, and spoken so that none shall hear: Will you have it so, shall I be yours?

Despite the jealous one, I will be true to you. So come, my joy, let us agree! Will you have it so?

[22] SONG *Crevez moy les yeulx*

Put out my eyes! Let me not see! Too much I fear beauty everywhere.

Beauty lies in wait to ravish all my joy out of the world. Put out my eyes! Let me not see!

God keep me from beauty, may our ways never meet!
Would not that be best? Put out my eyes! Let me not see!

[23] RONDEAU *Myn hert hath send Glad Hope in hys message** ·

Mine heart hath sent Glad Hope in his message
Unto comfort, pleasance, joy, and speed.
I pray to God that grace may him lead
Without letting or danger of passage.

In trust to find profit and advantage
Within short time to the help of his need,
Mine heart hath sent Glad Hope in his message
Unto comfort, pleasance, joy, and speed.

Till that he come, mine heart in hermitage
Of thought shall dwell alone (God give him meed!)
And of wishing of times shall him feed.
Glad Hope follow and speed well this voyage!
Mine heart hath sent Glad Hope in his message.

In his message: as his messenger. *pleasance:* pleasure. *speed:*
success. *letting:* hindrance. *meed:* reward. *of wishing of
times:* on longing for changed times. *speed well:* give success to.

* Written in English during his imprisonment in England.

François Villon
(1431 or '32 — after 1463)

[24] BALLADE: PRAYER TO OUR LADY WHICH
VILLON COMPOSED AT HIS MOTHER'S REQUEST
Dame des cieulx, regente terrienne

Lady of heaven, Queen of earth, Empress of the swamps
of Hell, receive me, your humble Christian woman; may I
be among your chosen though I was never worth anything.
Your virtues, my lady and mistress, are far greater than
my sins, without which virtues no soul can deserve to have
Heaven, and I mean what I say. In this faith I want to live
and die.

Tell your Son that I am his; may my sins be absolved by
him; may he forgive me as he did the Egyptian woman or
Theophilus the clerk, who was acquitted and absolved
through you though he had made a promise to the devil.
Keep me from ever doing that, Virgin who, suffering no
breach, bore the sacrament that is celebrated at mass. In
this faith I want to live and die.

I am a poor little old woman who knows nothing and has
never read a letter; in my parish church I see Paradise
painted, with harps and lutes, and a Hell where the damned
are boiled: the one makes me afraid, the other joyful and
happy. Give me the joy, high goddess, to whom all sinners
must turn full of faith, without hypocrisy or sloth. In this
faith I want to live and die.

Virgin, noble princess, you bore Jesus who reigns and who
is forever without end: he who, all powerful, taking our
weakness, left Heaven and came to save us, who gave to
death his most precious youth. Such is Our Lord, such I
acknowledge him. In this faith I want to live and die.

Virgin, noble princess, etc.: The initial letters of the first six lines
of the last stanza form the anagram V-I-L-L-O-N.

Anonymous

(12th century)

[25] ISOLT'S SONG WHEN SHE HEARD THAT
TRISTAN WAS DEAD *Li solex luist et clers et biaux**

The sun is shining, bright and beautiful, and I hear the sweet
song from birds singing in these bushes: they are making up
new songs all around me.

With these sweet songs, with these delights, and with love
that holds me in bonds, I begin my lay, I twine my song, to
cheer and comfort me dying.

Grieving, remembering my loss, I am tuning a song against
my death, making it without discords, a sweet, harmonious
lay.

Seeing my death upon me, I make a lay on it that will be
held dear; it cannot but touch all lovers that love has brought
me to my deathbed.

Happy, sad, singing, weeping, I pray to love and to God.
All lovers, come quickly! You shall see Isolt die singing.

I begin a lay of song and tears, I sing it and weep it. Singing
and weeping have brought me to that from which I shall
never return.

Tristan, my lover, now that I know you are dead, I curse
death that has put the world in grief for you. Only if its
jaws will close on me, too, will I take back that curse.

You are dead. Only if you could come back to life would
I wish to live. For you, my lover, I give myself to death.
The world will be well rid of me.

* From the "Romance of Tristan."

Anonymous

(13th — 14th centuries)

[26] SONG OF A CRUSADER'S LADY *Jherusalem, grant damage me fais*

Jerusalem, you do me great wrong; you have taken from me what most I loved. Believe me, I shall never love you more, for it is this that brings me my worst sorrow, and often I sigh and groan because of it, so that a little more and I should be on my way to God, who has banished me from the great joy that I had.

Fair sweet friend, how could you bear your great grief for me on the salt sea, when nothing that exists could lessen the great pain that has come into my heart? When I remember the sweet bright face that I used to kiss and fondle it is great wonder that I do not go mad.

So help me God, there is no escape for me; I must die, it is my fate. Yet I know that one who dies for love has but a short journey to God. Alas! I would rather set out on that journey, so that I may meet with my sweet lover, than remain here lost.

[27] WOMAN'S SONG *En dist camors est douce chose*

They say that love is sweet, but I know not its sweetness; it holds all joy, I have felt only its evil. Alas, my suffering never rests; ever I complain and cry out against it. It is twice the hurt to be beaten and not dare to cry, a grief spoken becomes less keen and is sooner assuaged.

I complain of him who has betrayed me and brought me to grief, for I who am still true to him now find no love in my lover. Often he kissed me, and I gave him my love. But there are those who kiss and love not at all; many a loving heart has been betrayed by kisses.

I believed that he loved me when he held me in his arms. When I was most stricken by love his words restored me;

at his voice I was cured even as Pyramus was when, dying, his side pierced by his own sword, he opened his eyes at Thisbe's name.

[28] GIRL'S SONG *Lasse, pour quoi refusai*

Alas! why did I refuse him who loved me so much? Long he had me in his thoughts and found no pity in me. Alas, that my heart is so hard! What can I say? I was out of my mind, I was stark mad when I refused him. *I will make it up to him however he pleases, if he will only listen to me!*

Truly I must call myself wretched and ill-fated, when he in whom there is nothing bitter but only sweetness gentle as dew begged me so sweetly and gained no pity: I was out of my mind when I did not love him. *I will make it up to him however he pleases, if he will only listen to me!*

He should have found pity when he pleaded for it; truly, I did a bad thing when I refused it to him. It has put me in great distress, I shall die if I am not given to him very soon. *I will make it up to him however he pleases, if he will only listen to me!*

To all those who have harmed him, God give an evil fate: may they have their eyes put out and their ears cut off! Then I shall feel no more grief. I will say to them: "You madmen, my joy is renewed twofold; and if I have done wrong, *I will make it up to him however he pleases, if he will only listen to me!*"

Song, linger not, but go to him in whom I so delight. Ask and implore him, in God's name, to come to me quickly. I will yield myself to him, he will soon find peace if so he wills, for I am suffering too greatly. *I will make it up to him however he pleases, if he will only listen to me.*

[29] DAWN SONG *Entre moi et mon amin*

On Tuesday I and my lover spent all night in a wood near Béthune, playing together till it dawned and the nightingale sang, saying, "Friend, we must go," and my lover answered softly: *"It is not day yet, O my delight with the sweet body; so help me love! the nightingale is telling us lies."*

Then he came close to me and I was not sullen; he kissed me three times and I gave him more than one, for he never displeased me. Then we wished that the night would last a hundred nights and that he need not say again: *"It is not day yet, O my delight with the sweet body; so help me love! the nightingale is telling us lies."*

[30] WOMAN'S DANCE SONG *Por coi me bat mes maris*

Why does my husband beat me, poor me!

I have done nothing to wrong him nor said anything to wrong him, I have only hugged my lover, all alone. *Why does my husband beat me, poor me!*

I cannot endure him, he will not let me be happy; I'll make him cry "Cuckoo!" and no mistake! *Why does my husband beat me, poor me!*

But I know what I will do and how I will be revenged on him: I will lie in bed with my lover, all naked. *Why does my husband beat me, poor me!*

[31] WOMAN'S DANCE SONG *Soufres, maris, et si ne vous anuit*

Let be, husband, and stop fretting: you shall have me tomorrow and my lover tonight.

I forbid you to say one word about it: *let be, husband, and stop fretting.*

The night is short; tomorrow morning you shall have me back again as soon as my lover has taken his pleasure. *Let be, husband, and stop fretting: you shall have me tomorrow and my lover tonight.*

[32] GIRL'S DANCE SONG *Toute seule passerai le vert boscage*

I will go through the green wood alone; I have no one to go with me.

If I have lost my lover by being scornful, *I will go through the green wood alone.*

I will send him a messenger to tell him that I will make it up to him. *I will go through the green wood alone; I have no one to go with me.*

[33] MOTET (Second Voice) *Cuers qui dort, il n'aimme pas*

A heart that sleeps does not love. I will never sleep, every day I will think faithfully of you, sweet, simple one, from whom I hope for joy and comfort. I will not sleep until I am in your soft arms.

[34] MOTET (Second Voice) *Je chantasse par revel*

I would sing gaily for her whom I have loved, but she has a new husband who has turned her against me, and he says he will have my skin and she will get a beating if I go there again. God! shall I not go again? Yes, I will! I will be the little mouse when I go in, no one shall see me.

[35] BALLAD *Volez vos que je vos chant*

Would you like me to sing you a charming song, all about love? No serf made it; a knight it was who made it, under the shade of an olive tree, in his dear lady's arms.

She had a shirt of linen and a white ermine-lined cloak and a tunic of silk; she had stockings of sword lily and shoes of mayflowers, close fitting.

She had a girdle of leaves that grow green in wet weather; her buttons were gold. Her chain-bag was of love, her pendants of flowers, a love gift.

She rode a mule: its shoes were silver, the saddle gold; on the crupper behind she had planted three rose bushes to give her shade.

So she goes down the meadow. Knights met her and greeted her courteously. "Beautiful lady, where were you born?" "I am from France the famous, of highest lineage.

"The nightingale is my father, who sings on the branch in the highest wood. The siren is my mother, who sings in the salt sea on the highest shore."

"Beautiful lady, well were you born; well are you allied, and of high lineage. Would to God our Father that you were given me as my wedded wife!"

[36] A MINSTREL'S WISHES *Quar eusse je .c. mile mars d'argent*

If only I had a hundred thousand silver pieces and as many of fine red gold, and if only I had a stock of oats and wheat, oxen and cows and lambs and sheep, and a thousand pounds to spend every year, and a castle so strong that no one could take it, with a freshwater port and a seaport!

And if only I could be openhanded and affable and clever, and young and healthy and gay and loved by everyone, and the best knight that ever lived so that no one would dare stand up to me, and could give whatever anyone asked for and grant everyone's wish, and enter Paradise whenever I chose!

If only I had strong, sparkling wine, a gilt cup, and meat and cake and fish, and a white tablecloth, and a cheese from a cool cellar strewn with fresh rushes, and if only I had a nice young unspoiled girl with a plump bottom that would give me something to hold on to, who would answer push for push and I would never get tired with her!

Anonymous
(15th century)

[37] LOVE SONG *L'amour de moi sy est enclose*

My love is set in a pretty garden, where roses and lilies of the valley grow and primroses too.

The garden is beautiful and pleasant, it has every kind of flower. It is a place to delight in both night and day.

Alas! there is nothing so sweet as this sweet nightingale that sings evening and morning; when he is tired, he rests.

I saw her the other day gathering violets on a green lawn —the most beautiful girl I ever saw and the most pleasing, I say.

I looked at her for a while: she was white as milk and gentle as a lamb, ruddy as a rose.

[38] LOVE SONG *J'ay veu la beauté m'amye*

I saw my lady's beauty shut up in a tower: would to the Virgin Mary that I were lord of it!

And that the sun had set, and day not yet dawned, and that, naked, I held you, my beauty, naked in my arms!

My heart, what will you do? Your pleasure is gone, your joy and your comfort. You cannot live without her.

[39] WAR SONG *Gentil duc de Lorraine, prince de grant renom*

Gentle Duke of Lorraine, prince of great fame, you are famed even beyond the mountains, you and your men-at-arms and all your companions. . . . Fire, fire, bombards, serpentines, and cannons!
"We are gentlemen, hold us for ransom!"

"You lie in your throats, you are nothing but robbers and rapers of women and house-burners. For that, you shall have the rope under your chins; and you shall hear matins sung by the birds, and you shall hear the Mass that the crows say!"

[40] HUSBAND'S SONG *Hellas! il est fait de ma vie*

Alas! my life is over: marriage has laid hold on me. To God I commend joy and gaiety, revel and singing.

I used to go reveling with gallant youths; now I sit by the hearth feeding my brats.

One howls, another cries, another calls me "Sir," another wakes me at dawn; I do not have a good hour or half-hour.

The biggest boy asks for a shirt, the littlest girl for a hat, and my wife howls and cackles, "Our Lady! what are we to do?"

Good God! be still, wife, be still! We will pray to Our Lord to give us bread in the oven to feed our brood.

[41] ALLEGORY *J'ay bien nourry sept ans ung joly gay*

For seven years I fed a bright jay in a cage. And when the first day of May came, my bright jay flew away.

It flew up to a pine tree. . . .

"Come back, come back, my bright jay, into your cage. I will make it of gold and silver for you, inside and out."

"No, I will not go into it, this year or next."

The jay flew straight to the woods; that was its right. It will not come back; freedom is its nature.

Nonsense Verses

[42] *Li sons d'un cornet*

The note of a trumpet was eating the heart of a thunder-
bolt with vinegar when a dead hobnail caught the course of
a star in a bird-trap. In the air there was a grain of rye, when
the barking of a roasting spit and the stump of a piece of
cloth found a worn-out fart and cut off its ear.

Fragments of Dance Songs

[43] (ca. A.D. 1050) *Equitabat Bovo per silvam frondosam*

Bovo was riding through the leafy wood;
With him he led fair Merswyn.
Why stand we? Why go we not?

[44] (ca. A.D. 1200) *Renaus et s'amie chevauche par un pre*

Rainaut is riding through a field with his lady;
He rides all night until bright day.
Now I shall never again have the joy of loving you.

Equitabat Bovo, etc.: Latin translation of the refrain of a French
or German dance song.

Refrains

(12th — 14th centuries)

[45] *Vante l'ore et li raim crollent*

The wind blows and the branches sway: they who love each other sleep sweet.

[46] *Deus, tant par vient sa joie lente*

God! how slowly his joy comes to him who longs for it!

[47] *Guis aime Aigline, Aigline aime Guion*

Guy loves Aigline, Aigline loves Guy.

[48] *Suis si pris*

I am so taken: sweet lover, let us rest!

[49] *Ja ne puis je durer sens vos*

I cannot go on without you: how do you go on without me?

[50] *A deu comans je mes amours*

I commend my love to God, may he keep her for me!

[51] *Senz amor ne puis durer*

I cannot go on without love, nor will I!

[52] *J'aim mult mels un poi de joie a demener*

I would rather take a little pleasure than have a thousand silver pieces and weep.

[53] *Tuit li amerous*

All lovers have gone to sleep: I am beautiful and blonde and I have no one.

[54] *Se j'avoie ameit un jor*

If I had loved for one day, I would say to all: Love is good.

[55] *J'ai apris a bien ameir*
I have learned to love truly: God grant me joy of loving.

[56] *Aleis soeif, si m'atendeis*
Go quietly and wait for me: your love has stolen my heart.

[57] *J' anmoins par les dois m' amie*
I lead my love by the hand: so I go more pleasantly.

[58] *Les mameletes me poignent*
My breasts itch: I am going to have a new lover.

[59] *A cui donrai jou mes amors*
To whom shall I give my love, sweetheart, if not to you?

[60] *Se je sui joliete*
If I am happy, let no one blame me for it.

[61] *Bon jor ait qui mon cuer a*
A good day to him who has my heart: he is not with me.

[62] *D'amors vient tote ma joie*
All my joy comes from love, and my happiness.

[63] *Dormez, qui n'amez mie*
Sleep, you who love not: I love, I cannot sleep.

[64] *Tote la joie que j'ai*
All the joy that I have comes to me from you.

[65] *Mes cuers est si jolis*
My heart is so happy! a little more, and it will fly away.

[66] *Que demandez vos*
What do you want when you have me? What do you want?
Have you not me?

III·GERMAN

Kürenberg
(fl. 1160; Austria)

[1] GIRL'S SONG *Swenne ich stân aleine*

When I stand alone in my shift and think of you, noble knight, my face reddens like the rose on the thorn and my heart is sad with many sorrows.

[2] ALLEGORY *Ich zôch mir einen valken*

I brought up a falcon for more than a year. When I had tamed it as I wanted it to be and had twined its feathers with gold, it soared up high and flew away to another country.

Later, I saw my falcon flying beautifully: on its feet it carried silken jesses and its feathers were all red-gold. God bring them together who would be lovers!

Dietmar von Eist

(died ca. 1170; Austria)

[3] COMPLAINT OF A LADY *Ez stuont ein frouwe alleine*

A lady stood alone, looking out over the heath, looking for her lover. She saw a falcon flying. "Well for you that you are a falcon! You fly wherever you will, you choose a tree in the woods that pleases you. So I did too: I chose a man, my eyes picked him out. Beautiful ladies are jealous of that. Alas! why will they not leave me my dear one? I never envied any of them her lover."

[4] LOVE SONG *Ûf der linden obene*

High up in a linden a little bird sang. It grew loud from the wood. And my heart rose to a place where it once was: I saw roses flowering there. They reminded me of the many thoughts that I have of a lady far away.

Meinloh von Sevelingen
(fl. 1180; Swabia)

[5] ON HIS LADY *Ich bin holt einer frouwen*

I am in love with a lady and well I know why. Since I began to serve her she has pleased me better and better. Dearer and dearer she is to me always, more and more beautiful. She pleases me very well. She is blest in all honorable qualities, she practices the highest virtues. If I died for love of her and then came back to life I would court her again.

Friedrich von Hausen

(ca. 1155 — 1190; Rhineland)

[6] CRUSADER'S SONG *Mîn herze und mîn lîp die wellent scheiden*

My heart and my body wish to part, they who have long traveled together. My body wants to fight the pagans. But my heart has chosen one lady above all the world. And ever since, I have been troubled because heart and body will no longer agree. My eyes did me this great harm. Only God can decide their quarrel.

I thought that I should be freed of this burden when I took the cross in God's honor. In duty, my heart should be with me there. But its loyalty forbids it. I should be a proper living man if my heart would give up its foolish resolve. Now I see well that it cares nothing to what end I come.

Since I cannot stop you, my heart, from leaving me in this sad plight, I pray to God that he will be pleased to send you to a place where you will be well received. Alas, what will befall you, poor heart! How dared you brave such a peril all alone? Who will help you out of your troubles as faithfully as I have always done?

The Emperor Heinrich VI
(1165 – 1197)

[7] TO HIS LADY *Ich grüeze mit gesange die süezen*

I greet in song the sweet lady whom I cannot and will not escape. Alas! it has been many days since I could greet her with my lips. Now whoever will sing this song before her whom I miss most bitterly, be it man or woman, will have greeted her from me.

Kingdoms and countries are under my rule when I am with that lovely lady; when I leave where she is, all my power and wealth are gone. Then longing and grief of soul is all that I count as mine. Thus in joy I rise and fall; and I think that, for love of her, I shall do even so to the grave.

Since I love her so dearly and ever bear her steadfastly both in my heart and my thoughts, sometimes with great grieving, what reward have I for my love? She seems to me so good and so beautiful that, sooner than give her up, I would give up my crown.

He commits a grave sin who does not believe that I could live many a joyful day even though a crown had never been set on my head. Without her I could not. If I lost her what should I have then? I should be unfit to please either man or woman. My best comfort would be exile and banishment.

Heinrich von Veldeke

(fl. 1185; Belgium)

[8] AGAINST WINTER *Swenn diu zît also gestât*

When the season comes that grants us flowers and grass
there is remedy for all that made my heart sad. The birds
would be happy if it were always summer as it once was.
Let the whole world be mine, yet would winter grieve me.

Albrecht von Johannsdorf

(born ca. 1160; Bavaria)

[9] ON HIS LADY *Saeh ich ieman der jaehe er waere
von ir komen*

If I saw anyone who said he had come from her, were I his
enemy I would greet him. If he had robbed me of all that I
have yet gained, he could make it up to me with his news.
Whoever speaks to me of her has me as his friend for a
whole year, even had he set fire to me.

Reinmar

(ca. 1155 — ca. 1210; Austria)

[10] ELEGY *Si jehent, der sumer der sî hie**

They say that summer is here, that joy has come, and that
I should be happy as I was before. Now speak and tell me
how! Death has robbed me of that which I can never recover. What use have I for the lovely season, when Leopold,
lord of all joys, lies in the ground, he whom I never saw sad
for a single day? In him the world has had a more grievous
loss than ever in any man before.

Poor woman, I was so happy when I thought of how my
well-being lay in him. That I shall never have that again
makes the rest of my life a sorrow, no matter what may
befall me. The mirror of my joys is lost. He whom I had
chosen for my eyes' summer festival, alas! I must be without
him. When they told me he was dead, my blood welled
from my heart into my soul.

My dear lord's death has forbidden me joy, so that I may
never have it again. Since there is no remedy henceforth but
that I must struggle with grief and my mourning heart be
full of care, she who weeps for him is I. For he, blessed man,
was my protection as long as he lived. Now he is gone.
What should I do here? Be merciful to him, Lord God! A
more virtuous guest never entered your service.

* Composed for the widow of Leopold VI of Austria.

Heinrich von Morungen
(fl. 1190 — 1218; Thuringia)

[11] EXCHANGE AFTER A PARTING AT DAWN
Owê, sol aber mir iemer mê

"Alas, will it ever again shine on me through the night, her well-made body, whiter than snow? It deceived my eyes: I thought it must be the bright moonlight. *Then it dawned.*"

"Alas, will he ever again wait for day to dawn here? May night pass for us so that we need not complain, 'Alas! now it is dawn,' even as he complained when last he lay beside me! *Then it dawned.*"

"Alas, she kissed me countless times in my sleep. Then her tears fell one after the other. Yet I comforted her so that she stopped weeping and took me in her arms. *Then it dawned.*"

"Alas, he often lost himself in gazing at me! When he uncovered me he wanted to look at me in my poor nakedness. I wondered that he never tired of it. *Then it dawned.*"

[12] TO HIS LADY *Frouwe, wilt du mich genern*

Lady, if you would save me look at me only a little. I can no longer defend myself, I must lose my life. I am sick, my heart is sore. Lady, this has been the doing of my eyes and your red mouth.

Lady, look on my misery before I lose my life. There is a word that you have spoken against me. Change it, lovely lady. Always you say: "No no no" and "No no, no no, no no no!" That breaks my heart in two. Can you not some time say: "Yes yes, yes yes, yes yes yes"? That is what my heart asks.

Walther von der Vogelweide

(ca. 1170 — ca. 1230; Austria)

[13] GIRL'S SONG *Under der linden*

Under the linden tree in the fields where we two had our bed, there you could find both flowers and grass beautifully broken. At the edge of the wood in the valley—*tandaradei*— the nightingale sang beautifully.

I came walking to the meadow; but my lover was there before me. There I found such a greeting that I am happy forevermore. Did he kiss me? Why, a thousand times—*tandaradei*—see how red my mouth is!

Then he made a fine bed of flowers. If anyone comes by the same path, he will laugh heartily even now. He can tell from the roses—*tandaradei*—where my head lay.

If any one knew (God forbid!) that he lay beside me, I should be ashamed. What he did with me, may no one ever find it out except him and me and a little bird—*tandaradei!* But it, I think, will not tell.

[14] GNOMIC POEM *Mehtiger got, du bist so lanc und bist so breit*

Mighty God, thou art so long and art so broad! Let us consider this, lest we lose our labor. Thine are both boundless power and eternity. This I know in myself, whatever another may think of it. It is now, as it always was, inaccessible to our senses. Thou art too great, thou art too small, it is inconceivable. He is a fool who spends his days and nights over it. Would he know what has never been said in sermon or dogma?

Kristan von Hamle

(fl. ca. 1225; Thuringia)

[15] SIR MEADOW *Ich wolte daz der anger sprechen solte*

I wish that the meadow could speak, like the parrot behind its glass, and would tell me truly how sweet it was to him this season when my lady gathered flowers from him and her lovely feet stirred his green grass.

Sir Meadow, what joy you must have felt when my lady came walking and reached out her white hands for your lovely flowers! Grant me, Sir Green Field, that I may set my feet there where my lady walked.

Sir Meadow, pray that she on whom my heart is set may cure me of my grief. So will I wish that she may walk on you again this season barefooted; so may snow never harm you. If she will send me a loving greeting my heart will grow as green as your clover.

behind its glass: in its cage.

Neidhart

(ca. 1180 — ca. 1250; Bavaria)

[16] A VILLAGE DANCE *Sinc, ein guldîn huon*

"Sing, golden cockerel; I will give you grain!" That made me happy at once. For I am always glad to sing to gain her favor. Even so a promise of good makes a fool happy for a year. If hers should come true no man's spirits were ever so high as mine would be. Will she, in her mercy, transform my grieving? My plight is pitiful indeed.

Clear away the stools and chairs! Have the trestles carried out! Today we shall dance till we are tired. Open up the room! it will be cooler and the wind can blow softly on the girls through their bodices. As soon as the leaders stop singing, you will all be asked to step another little court dance with us to the fiddle.

Listen! I hear dancing in the room. Come on, lads! There is a great crowd of village women inside. There we saw many a round dance. When the two fiddles stopped it was a delight for the village lads; they took turns singing for the dancers. The noise came through the windows. Adelhalm only dances between two girls.

Did you ever see a peasant so trim as he is? By Christ! he is always first in the dance. His sword has a belt two spans wide. He thinks his new doublet is very fine; it is made of twenty-four pieces of cloth; the sleeves come down over his hands. His clothes are what you would find on a vain fool.

Everything he is wearing is countrified. They tell me he is courting Engelbolt's daughter Ave. But I think his courtship is pure loss. She is a girl fit for a count to love. So, to give him a quiet word of advice, let him go look elsewhere. What he would gain here he could carry to Mainz in his eye!

Gottfried von Neifen

(ca. 1200 — ca. 1255; Swabia)

[17] AT THE SPRING *Rife und anehanc*

Black frost and white have seized on the field so that its brightness has become a pitiful sight. And the song of the birds that sang for joy—now they are silent. I grieve for the wood too: it is stripped bare. Yet she who fetches water from the spring in jugs can cause a keener grief. My thought is all of her.

I carried her jug for her when she came from the spring. I was happy, seeing her loveliness. Because she let me help her all my sorrow was gone. Fondly she spoke, the lovely girl: "I am in trouble, it is your fault. My mistress is cruel to me, and I have to put up with it. Yesterday she beat me five times because of you."

"Do as I say, I will get you out of your trouble. Come away with me, and you will be safe from her anger." "That cannot be. Sooner would I die! I should lose my mistress's love forever. She owes me a shilling and a shift besides. I know very well that I should never see them. As soon as I get them I will be quick to help you."

[18] GIRL'S SONG *Sol ich disen sumer lanc*

Am I to be burdened with children all this summer? I would rather be dead! It kills all my joy. If I cannot go dancing at the linden, oh what misery! *Rockaby baby, sleep, sleep— when will day dawn? Hushaby baby, I will rock you.*

Nurse, as you love me, take the baby and make it stop crying. Rid me of my burden; only you can free me from my grief. *Rockaby baby, sleep, sleep—when will day dawn? Hushaby baby, I will rock you.*

[19] BALLAD *Ez fuor ein büttenaere*

A cooper traveled far in a foreign land. He was so fit for love that, wherever he found women, he was glad to ply his trade.

The genial host asked him what he could do. "I am a cooper; if anyone wants, I hoop his barrel for him."

He brought his hoops and his adz; with his traveling about he earned a good living and could carry good tools.

She took his adz in her hand, and straight it was. "Savior!" she said, "it was God who sent you."

When they had hooped the host's barrel all round and underneath too, she said: "You are no sluggard, my barrel was never hooped better!"

Marner

(ca. 1220 — ca. 1270; Swabia)

[20] AGAINST A RIVAL POET *Wê dir, von Zweter Regimâr**

Woe to you, Reinmar von Zweter, you refurbish many an old thought, you split a hair like a mite; for you a penny becomes a pound—if your prophesying does not deceive you. For you a day becomes a year, a wild wolf becomes a dog, a goose a cuckoo, a bustard a starling; to hear you tell it, a stag can spin. What proof have you of that? A lie passes your lips like downright truth. You have made fish cough and given crabs a harvest field. In short there are three monstrous beasts in you: cupidity, hatred, and envy. You thief of tunes, you brew beer without malt. Lick the plate clean! The man who is dearest to you is a sponger who is forever telling lies to his betters.

* See Reinmar von Zweter's "Nonsense Verse" (No. 21).

Reinmar von Zweter

(ca. 1200 — ca. 1255; Rhineland)

[21] NONSENSE VERSE *Ich quam geriten in ein lant*

I came riding into a land on a blue goose. There I found marvels. A crow and a hawk were catching pigs in a brook, a hare led two winds, a bear was hunting a falcon and caught it high in the air, flies were playing chess, I saw two ants building a tower. A stag sat spinning fine silk, a wolf was guarding lambs in the field, a crab flew against a pigeon on a bet and won a pound from her, a cock bit three great giants to death. If this is true, a donkey makes hats.

Alexander
(ca. 1239 — ca. 1290; Southern Germany)

[22] ALLEGORY *Hie vor dô wir kinder wâren*

Long ago, when we were children and it was the time of the
year when we could run in the meadows, back and forth
from one to another, we sometimes found violets where
now cattle roam.

Well I remember that we sat among the flowers, trying to
decide which was the prettiest. Then our childish bravery
was bright in the dance with fresh wreaths. So time passes
away.

See us looking for strawberries, from the pines to the
beeches, over stocks and stones, so long as the sun shone.
Then a forester shouted through the branches, "Now, children, go home!"

We all got stained with red from picking strawberries. That
was fun for us children. Often we heard our herdsman calling and shouting, "Children, there are many snakes here!"

One child went into the tall grass, he had a fright and cried
out, "Children, a snake ran in there, it bit our little play-
mate; his wound will never be healed, he will waste away
in suffering."

"Out of the wood now! Hurry, or it will befall you as I
tell you: If you do not make your way out of the wood
while it is day, you will be too late and your joy will turn to
sorrow.

"Do you not know that five virgins dallied late in the field
until the king shut the door? Their woe and their loss was
great, for the prison guards stripped off their dresses and
they stood naked."

"Out of the wood now! . . .": The speaker is again the forester
(cf. stanza 3).

Steinmar von Klingenau

(ca. 1250 — ca. 1294; Switzerland)

[23] DAWN SONG *Ein kneht der lac verborgen*

A farm boy lay secretly sleeping beside a maid until day dawned. The herdsman called: "Up! Let the cattle out!" That startled the maid and her dear companion.

He must needs leave the straw and part from his love. He dared not linger, he took her in his arms. The girl saw the hay that covered him fly up into the light.

It made her laugh, and her eyes closed. So sweetly could he play the bed game with her in the early morning. Who ever saw such happiness without a stick of furniture?

Duke Johan of Brabant

(ca. 1254 — 1294; Netherlands)

[24] MAY *Eenes meienmorghens vroe*

Early one May morning I rose to take my pleasure in a lovely little flower garden. There I found three young ladies. One sang first, then another: "*Harbalorifa, harbaharbalorifa, harbalorifa!*"

When I saw the lovely plants in the little flower garden and heard the sweet voices of those charming girls, my heart was glad, so that I had to sing after them: "*Harbalorifa, harbaharbalorifa, harbalorifa!*"

Then I greeted the loveliest of them as they stood there, and put my arms around her. I was going to kiss her on the lips. But she said: "Let be! let be! let be! *Harbalorifa, harbahar-balorifa, harbalorifa!*"

Johannes Hadlaub

(ca. 1280 — ca. 1340; Switzerland)

[25] ON HIS LADY *Als ich sach sî triuten wol ein kindelîn*

When I saw her fondling a little child my heart was reminded of love. She put her arms around him and held him close and I was filled with loving thoughts. She took his face in her white hands and pressed it to her mouth and her bright cheeks. Alas! she even kissed him!

He did just what I would have done; I saw him embrace her too. He acted as if he understood all the joy of her, it seemed to me—he was so happy. I could not leave without envying him. I thought: "Oh, might I be that child so long as she will love him!"

I watched for the child to leave her, then I took him to me lovingly. It had given me such pleasure when she had held him close and I was so happy for him. I embraced him as she had done and kissed him where she had kissed him. How that went to my heart!

People say that I am not as truly in grief for her as they have heard; they say that I am well, that I would be sick and would look it if the bond of love grieved me so much. That they do not see it in me despite my suffering is because of a good hope, which has helped me until now. If I lost it, I should die.

Anonymous

(12th — 15th centuries)

[26] GIRL'S SONG *Mich dunket nicht sô guotes*

I think nothing so good or to be praised as bright roses and the love of my man. The little birds sing in the wood; it makes many hearts glad. If my darling does not come to me, I can have no joy of the summer.

[27] GIRL'S SONG *Dû bist mîn, ich bin dîn*

You are mine, I am yours—be sure of that! You are locked up in my heart and the key is lost. You must stay there forever.

[28] WOMAN'S SONG *Mir hât ein ritter, sprach ein wîp*

A lady spoke: "A knight has served me as I willed. Before the season changes, he must have his reward. Winter and snow seem to me lovely flowers and clover when I hold him in my arms. Were all the world against it, he should have his will of me."

[29] LOVE SONG *Kume kum, geselle mîn*

Come, come, my darling; I wait for you sorely. I wait for you sorely; come, come, my darling.

Sweet rose-red mouth, come and make me well. Come and make me well, sweet rose-red mouth.

[30] LOVE SONG *Bis willkommen, lieb junkfräwlin zart*

Welcome, dear sweet girl! I have been so long without you! No time ever seemed so long to me before. Be sure that my heart never forgot you.

"God bless you a hundred thousand times," I say, in all honesty. Ever since longing for you, my comfort, has set me on fire, I never tire of making that wish.

However far I have been from you, my highest treasure, know that my heart and mind and thought are with you. If I were to live a thousand years, the longer the better—if you love me!

IV·ITALIAN

Francesco d'Assisi

(died 1226)

[1] CANTICLE OF PRAISE *Altissimu onnipotente bon signore*

Most high omnipotent good Lord, thine are praises, glory, honor, and every blessing.

To thee alone, Most High, do they belong, and no man is worthy to name thee.

Praised be thou, my Lord, by all thy creatures, especially master brother sun, who dawns and thou lightest us by him, and he is beautiful and shining with great brightness; of thee, Most High, he bears significance.

Praised be thou, my Lord, by sister moon and the stars; thou didst create them in the sky, bright and precious and beautiful.

Praised be thou, my Lord, by brother wind and by air and cloud and calm and every kind of weather, by which thou givest sustenance to thy creatures.

Praised be thou, my Lord, by sister water, who is most useful and humble and precious and chaste.

Praised be thou, my Lord, by brother fire, by whom thou lightest the night, and he is beautiful and merry and most robust and strong.

Praised be thou, my Lord, by sister our mother earth, who sustains and fosters us and brings forth various fruits with colored flowers and grass. . . .

Praise ye and bless my Lord and give thanks and serve him with great humility.

Giacomo da Lentino

(fl. 1230)

[2] DIALOGUE *Dolcie coninciamento*

A sweet beginning! I sing for the most accomplished lady from Agri to Messina—so I think her—and the most beautiful. O brightest morning star! When you appear before me your sweet looks set my heart on fire.

"My sweet lord, if you are on fire, what am I supposed to do? You scold me yourself if you see me going about saying that you have made me fall in love. You have pierced my heart, but with a wound that does not show. Remember sometimes how, holding you in my arms—ah, those sweet kisses!"

And I too, kissing and being kissed, took great delight in her who loved me, she of the blonde hair and silver face. Frankly she told me of her state, hiding nothing, saying: "I will love you and never betray you my whole life long."

Nor I in all my life will ever betray you, my dear, despite his evil tongue who speaks of betrayal.

"And I will love you, despite that cruel one. May God make him wretched! Let him dance at no maypole! He is so ill-conditioned that even in summer he is cold."

Pier della Vigna
(ca. 1180 – 1249)

[3] TO HIS LADY *Amore in cui disio ed o speranza*

Love, in which is my desire and my hope, has given me my reward, beautiful lady, in you. I look for joy to come, yet await fit time and season. Like a man gone to sea hoping to begin his voyage, and the wind blows timely and he sets sails and hope never deceives him—even so do I, my lady, when I come before you.

Oh that I could come to you, loving heart, like the thief, unknown and unseen! What joyous good fortune I should count it if love granted me such a favor! How eloquently I would speak to you, lady, to tell you that I have long loved you more tenderly than ever Pyramus loved Thisbe and will love you as long as I live!

It is love of you that keeps me in desire and gives me hope with great joy, for I care not if I suffer melancholy or torture, thinking of the hour when I shall come to you. For if I delay too long, O perfumed mouth, I think that I must perish and you will lose me. Therefore, beautiful lady, if you love me beware lest I die in hope of you.

In hope of you I live, my lady, and my heart longs for you always and I think the hour is growing late for true love to bring me into your heart. I wait for it to be your pleasure that I set sail toward you, O rose, and come to port where my heart will find rest in your courtesy.

My song, carry these plaints to her who holds my heart in possession, tell her my sufferings and how I am dying for love of her, and let her send me a messenger to tell me how I can comfort the love I bear her; and if I have offended her in anything let her punish me with whatever penance she will.

Frederick II

(1194 – 1250)

[4] TO HIS LADY *Oi llasso, nom pensai*

Alas, I did not think that separation from my lady would seem so hard. Ever since I went away it has seemed that I must die, remembering her sweet companionship. I have never endured such anguish as I did when I was on board the ship. And now I believe that I shall surely die if I do not return to her very soon.

Everything that I see is so irksome to me that I can find rest nowhere. Desire so holds me that I have no peace and even laughter and gaiety seem evils. When I remember her sweet ways all delights flee from my mind. And I can never expect to be consoled except where my sweet lady is.

God, what a fool I was when I went from where I had been so honored! Dearly am I paying for it! I melt like snow when I think that another has her in his power. It seems a thousand years away, the day when I shall return to you, my lady; the evil thought so torments me that it lets me neither laugh nor enjoy myself.

Happy song, go to the flower of Syria, to her who holds my heart in prison. Ask that most loving lady, of her courtesy, to remember her servant, who will suffer from love of her until he has done all that she commands him to do. And beg her, of her goodness, to deign to remain loyal to me.

Odo delle Colonne

(13th century)

[5] GIRL'S SONG *Oi llassa, namorata*

A girl in love, alas! I will tell my life, saying always what love bids me. I have done nothing wrong, yet I am filled with pains enough for one whom I love and want and have him not at my will as I used to have, so that I suffer anguish, and then pride guides me and splits my heart.

Alas! poor wretch that I am, how love has taken me! For he who has conquered me calls me his love. His beauty has robbed me of joy and laughter and put me in pain and great torment; I shall never be well again, I think, unless death succors me; I wait for it to come and take me from this fate.

Alas! when he had me in secret he said, "O my life, I am more content with you than if I had the world at my will and were lord of it." And now he disdains and denies me. It seems that he has another love. O God! who is she who is my rival for him? May she die stabbed treacherously and unrepentant!

O evil, cruel Fate! free me from this suffering, help me quickly, as I shall perish if my lord does not deign to have me, for his speech was sweet to me and he has made me love him beyond measure. Now his heart has changed; consider how hard that is for me! I am in despair, I abandon myself to Fate.

Go to him, cunning song, in his good fortune. Stab him in the heart if you find him disdainful; no! do not stab him so hard that you hurt him too much. But stab her who holds him; kill her without fail. Then, I know, he of the bright face will come to me, and I shall be free of torment and have joy and delight.

Rinaldo d'Aquino

(fl. 1230)

[6] GIRL'S SONG *Ormai quando flore*

Now that the flowers are out and fields and stream banks show green, the birds make merry among the leaves, singing as their way is in this fresh, leafy springtime, each inviting to perfect joy.

The fragrance of the flowers and the birds' songs urge me to love. When dawn comes I hear their gentle loves and the beautiful, sweet new verses and tunes that they vie in making, each trying to outdo all the others in the coppice.

As I listen to the lark and the nightingale singing of spring my heart grows gentle with love. And then I know all the better that this heart is wood of another kind, for it never stops burning. Seeing the new shadow under the trees, of this I am sure: the love that bends me will soon be satisfied.

It bends me, for I am loved. And though I never loved before, the season fills me with love and makes me wonder if I should take pity on a youth who worships me and who, I know, is suffering great pain and torment for me.

Therefore I pray to love that sweeps me as the wind a leaf not to take from me what, gone, will take away my good name, and to be content with me. For he who longs to enjoy my love fully and in secret is not yet satisfied.

Giacomino Pugliese

(13th century)

[7] ON THE DEATH OF HIS LADY *Mortte, perché m'ài fatta sì gran guerra*

Death, why have you made such great war upon me, taking my lady from me, she for whom I grieve? You have laid her dead in the ground, she the flower of beauties, so that I love not the world nor will have it. Churlish Death, who has no pity! You break love and steal joy and give sorrow. You have changed my joy to great sadness, taking from me the delight and the joy that I was wont to have.

I was wont to have contentment and play and laughter, more than any other knight alive. Now my lady has gone to Paradise and taken with her my sweet hope. She has left me in grief and with sighs and tears, she has turned me from play and songs and sweet companionship. Now I no longer see her nor stand before her, nor does she give me sweet looks as she was wont.

O God! why hast thou put me in such despair? For I am lost, I know not where I am, since thou hast taken my sweet hope, parted our sweetest companionship. Alas! I am nowhere, it seems! My lady, who has your face? Where is your gentility imprisoned? Who has taken your true heart from me, my lady?

Where is my lady and her gentility? her beauty and great knowledge? her sweet smile and lovely speech? her grace and her courtesy? My lady, through whom I was ever in joy—I see her no longer, neither day nor night, no longer do I rejoice, as once I did, in her countenance.

If the Kingdom of Hungary were mine, with Greece and Germany as far as France, and the great treasure of Santa Sophia, it could not make good so great a loss as I have suffered. For, alas! on that day when my lady went away, departing this life amid great sorrow, she left me sighs and griefs and tears and she has never sent me any joy to comfort me.

If I could do as I would, lady, I would tell God, who does all things, to let us be together day and night. But God's will be done, as it pleases him. I remember that when she was with me she often called me "sweet lover," and now she does not, since God took her and keeps her with him. May his power be with you, beautiful one, and his peace!

Compagnetto da Prato

(13th century)

[8] DIALOGUE *Per lo marito c'ho rio*

"It is all because my husband is a brute that love has come into my heart, bringing me great happiness and comfort for the evil that I suffer with him. I had no such thought until his cruelty set me to loving; now I have a true lover who keeps me in great joy.

"You beat me, jealous brute; you delight in giving me pain. But the more you wrong me, the more you make me love him. You upbraided me with a man when there was no love between us. But as soon as you put him into my head, I fell in love with him. And so you contrived your own downfall.

"My lover argues with me: he asks me if I love him truly, since he won me because I was in that evil one's power. My lover, you won me because I hated my husband, not for love. But since you have had me, your sweetness has so entered my heart that all my evil has changed to good.

"My lover, I complain to you of an old hag who is my neighbor. She has discovered that I love you, and now her evil tongue never stops. She rages and reproaches me with you. She puts me to greater torment than my husband does, she gives me no peace."

"My lady, as I honor you, never pay attention to any old woman. For they make war on love so that no one will notice theirs. Old women are an evil race. Do not be dismayed. For our sweet true love will not change for them. May God send them to the fire!"

She says: "By God! I swear to you by my loyalty that there is nothing for which I would stop loving you. If I complain to you of this one misfortune never suppose that I am thinking of another love but only of doing whatever will please you."

Ruggieri Pugliese

(13th century)

[9] DIALOGUE *L'altro ier fui 'n parlamento*

Two days ago I had speech with her whom I have loved. Grievously she complained to me that she is being forced to marry against her will. She said: "My lover, I beg you: pity me and help me! For you are my god on earth; I have put myself in your hands. Because of you, I cannot bear him.

"In truth I should be dead, for my heart is torn from my body. I see my father making ready to do this wrong to me. You who are my lord and god, advise me, help me against this man who is taking me by force. O that I could see him lying dead before me! He wants nothing but my harm.

"My lover, take me away from him, save me from this misery! Send me somewhere—that is what I want. I have no power over my father, who is murdering me. All the help he gives me is to turn my joy into misery and keep me from doing what is good."

"Lady, your marriage grieves me to the heart. Yet it must be. Reason forbids anything else, of that I am sure. For I love you so well that I would not have you commit a fault for which I am in dread that people would blame you. I say it in all truth.

"Many a lady has a husband whom she hates. She treats him pleasantly and courteously, but loves him none the more for that. So I would have you do; and great joy will reward you. When I hold you naked in my arms all your unhappiness will leave you. See to it that you do as I say."

Guido delle Colonne
(ca. 1210 — after 1277)

[10] TO HIS LADY *Ancor che l'aigua per lo foco lassi*

Though water loses its great coldness through fire, it would not change that natural property if there were not some vessel between them; instead, in no long time either the fire would be quenched or the water be dried up. But because of what is between them they both continue to exist. Even so, accomplished lady, has love displayed its fiery power in me; for without love I was cold water and ice but love has fired me with an enveloping flame, such that I should be consumed if you, sovereign creature, were not interposed between me and love, which causes fire to be born from snow.

A snow image may he well be called who feels not the heat of love; though he is alive he is incapable of joy. Love is a spirit of fire that cannot be seen but makes itself felt only by sighs in him who is a lover. Even so, honorable lady, my great sighing should make you certain that I am wrapped in love's flame. I do not know how I survive, such hold has it taken on me. But of this I am sure: many other lovers have been done to death by love, none of whom loved as much and as intensely as I.

I love you so much that, thinking of your beauty, my failing spirit is torn from me a thousand times in an hour. And desire lays hold of my heart, increases my longing, takes my thoughts like a whirlwind, for it never wearies. O white and rosy joy, hope of good to come sustains me, and if I languish I cannot die. For as long as you are alive I could not perish, though hunger and thirst should torture my body; I have only to think of your joyous self and it fills me with such strength that I forget death.

I do not believe the spirit within me is that which I had before; for I should already be dead from having suffered such evils so long. The spirit I have, which gives me life and motion, I believe is yours, which is in my breast and lives with me in great joy and gladness. For when last I left your presence, I became aware that, when I was looking upon your fresh, bright face of love, your beautiful eyes made me two in that moment, for, looking upon me, they gave me a secret spirit of love, which makes me love far more than any other ever loved, so I think.

The magnet, so say the learned, could not draw iron by force if the air between did not enable it to do so. Though the magnet is stone, no other stones have such ability to draw, because the power has not been accorded them. Even so, my lady, love found that it could not draw me to itself except through you. To be sure, there are ladies in plenty, but not one of them all by whom I would ever be moved except by you, in whose lovely self lie the force and the power. Therefore I implore love to help me.

Guittone d'Arezzo

(ca. 1230 — 1294)

[11] SPIRITUAL DANCE *Vegna, vegna chi vol gio-cundare*

Come, come, all who would rejoice, and join in the dance.

Come, come, let them rejoice and be glad, they who love thee, from whom alone is all joy; and they who love thee not, Love, let them not presume to rejoice in what is sorrow. Consent, consent! Guilty is he who scorns thy joyousness.

There is no joy nor true comfort save in loving thee, Jesus my dear spouse; so lovable and pleasing art thou that with thee all sweet and all bitter are sweet. Persist, persist every heart in loving thee, disdaining all else.

Prophets and saints invite us, Love, to love thee joyously and sing songs and hymns in praise of thee in whom all praise and glory appear. Constrain, constrain us, Love, ever to do what right teaches.

O life of life by which I live, living without which I die and live in death, and joy by which I rejoice and am joyful, rejoicing without which my lot is all griefs, deign, deign to wed my soul and make it wholly worthy of thee.

O true joy of my spirit, may my soul rejoice in thee with all delight, so that I may see thy face and hear thy voice, there where perfect joy is eternal. Reign, reign in me, making me to reign as the just man reigns.

O come, come and rejoice, brides of my Lord and ladies mine, be happy with all happiness, loving him with a pure heart every day. Scorn, scorn, good heart, all that is not fitting for your Lord.

Persist, persist, they who seek pain, in pain; and come they not to thy dance!

Jacopone da Todi

(ca. 1230 – 1306)

[12] BALLATA: A FOOL FOR CHRIST *Senno me par e cortesia*

I hold it wisdom and courtesy to be a fool for the fair Messiah.

If any will be a fool for God, I hold it such great wisdom that Paris cannot show such high philosophy.

He who is a fool for Christ appears sad and troubled; but he is a past master in natural philosophy and theology.

He who is foolish for Christ seems mad to the world; anyone who has not known what it is thinks him out of the right road.

Whoever will enter this school will find new doctrine; he who does not try folly does not know how good it is.

Whoever will enter this dance finds immeasurable love: a hundred days' indulgence to him who mocks him!

Whoever seeks honor is not worthy of Jesus' love, for he hung on the cross between two thieves.

Whoever seeks shame will quickly be the gainer. He need not go back to Bologna to learn any other science.

Rustico Filippi

(ca. 1235 — ca. 1295)

[13] SONNET: WIFE TO HUSBAND *Oi dolcie mio marito Aldobrandino*

"O my sweet husband Aldobrandino, do send Piletto back his doublet, and right away. He is such a bright, well-mannered lad—you must not believe what you have been told about him. And stop going around with your head hanging. Because you are not a cuckold—I solemnly deny it! He only came here like any loving neighbor, to sleep in our bed with us.

"So enough of this keeping his doublet! send it back to him at once. He will never come here again, unless you want him to, now that he knows how you feel about it. He never undresses in our bed. You ought to keep quiet instead of making all this fuss. He never did anything to me that I mind his having done."

Compiuta Donzella

(13th century)

[14] SONNET: COMPLAINT *A la stasgione che 'l monddo folglia e fiora*

In the season when the world leafs and flowers, joy grows for all true lovers; together they go to the gardens where birds sing sweetly. All young men who are not churls fall in love and vie with one another in serving; and every girl knows only joy. But for me there are grief and tears.

For my father has brought me to dismay, and often he hurts me cruelly. He means to give me a husband against my will. And I neither want that nor can I abide it. So, every hour, I am in great torment, and neither flowers nor leaves can cheer me.

Cecco Angiolieri

(ca. 1260 — ca. 1312)

[15] SONNET: LOVE SONG *Quanto un granel di panico e minore*

By as much as a millet seed is smaller than the greatest mountain I have ever seen; by as much as a good gold florin is better than any baser coin; by as much worse as it is to me to suffer pain—and I suffer it—than to be rid of it: by so much are the pains of love greater than I could ever have believed.

Yet now I believe in them, for I undergo them in such fashion that, by my soul! I wish I were still a novice in this love. But as for stopping loving, I have as much power to do it as the chick in the egg has of hatching out before its time comes.

Guido Cavalcanti

(ca. 1259 — 1300)

[16] BALLATA: PASTORAL *In un boschetto trova' pasturella*

In a little wood I found a shepherdess more beautiful, I thought, than any star.

She had blonde hair in ringlets and eyes full of love and a rosy face. She was tending sheep with her crook, and her bare feet were bathed in dew. She sang as if she were in love, and every beauty graced her.

I greeted her at once with words of love and asked if she were in company. And she answered me sweetly that she was all alone there in the wood. And she said: "Know that when a bird pipes, my heart longs to have a lover."

When she had thus told me her state and I heard birds singing in the wood, I said to myself: "Now is the time to have joy of this shepherdess." I asked her if she would be pleased to show me mercy so far as to kiss me and embrace me.

She took me lovingly by the hand and said that she had given me her heart. She led me under a leafy shade where I saw flowers of every color. And there I felt such joy and sweetness that I seemed to see the God of Love himself.

Immanuel Romano

(ca. 1265 — ca. 1330)

[17] SONNET: SATIRE *In stesso non mi conosco, ogn' om oda*

I am far from certain, I confess, that the only thing to be is a Ghibelline. In Rome I side with both the Colonnesi and the Orsini, and I am equally happy whichever of them wins. In Tuscany I am for the Guelfs; in Romagna I am as much a Ghibelline as Zappetino. I am a bad Jew; but I am neither a Saracen nor have I any intention of going over to the Christians.

Yet I am more than willing to observe some part of every religion. To wit: the way the Christians eat and drink; good Moses' scanty abstinence; and best Mahomet's lustfulness. For he has no creed from the waist down.

Dante Alighieri

(1265 — 1321)

[18] SESTINA: LOVE SONG *Al poco giorno e al gran cerchio d'ombra*

To this short daylight and great circling of shadow I have come, alas! and to the whitening of hills when color goes from the herbage; yet not for that does my desire change its green, so is it rooted in this hard stone that speaks and hears as if it were a lady.

So, too, this new lady remains as frozen as snow in shadow. For she is moved no more than stone by the sweet season that warms the hills and makes them turn from white to green, covering them with flowers and herbage.

When her head wears a garland of herbage, she empties our mind of every other lady; for that mingling of crisped gold and green is so beautiful that Love comes to linger in their shadow, Love that has imprisoned me among little hills more closely than lime locks stone.

Her beauty has more virtue than any stone and the wound she gives cannot be cured by any herb; I have fled over plains and hills to escape from such a lady, yet such is her light that nothing can shade me from it, neither mountain nor wall nor spray of green.

I saw her once dressed in green, so fashioned that she would have filled a stone with the love that I bear even to her shadow; so that I wished her in a fair field of herbage, as much in love as ever was a lady, and all around should be most high hills.

But the streams will return to the hills before that wood so soft and green catches fire, as fair lady does, from me, who would sleep on stone all my life and go feeding on herbs, only to look upon the place where her garments cast their shadow.

Even when the hills throw their blackest shadow this young lady makes it vanish under a lovely green, like a stone concealed under herbage.

Pieraccio Tedaldi

(ca. 1290 — ca. 1350)

[19] TAILED SONNET: THE DEBTOR *Oggi abbian lunedi, come tu sai*

Today, as you know, is Monday; tomorrow, as usual, Tuesday. The next day is Wednesday; then, inevitably, comes Thursday. I know that you know the next, for meat is nowhere eaten on it. The next, as I remember, is Saturday. Then comes the day on which no one goes shopping.

On every one of them you have told me that you would pay me what you owe me—and then you tell me that you are too busy. You are less busy than I am, and your promises, I find, are worthless, they have no more substance than nothing at all.

So answer me: Do you think I will be repaid before Judgment Day? If not, I renounce my claim.

Niccolò Soldanieri

(fl. 1350 — 1370)

[20] MADRIGAL: ALLEGORY *Un bel girfalco scese alle mie grida**

A beautiful gyrfalcon came from the sky to my call, dropping down like a plummet onto my arm, as love willed and the desire of its wings.

I set it on a perch, and when it had ruffled its throat feathers it soared up higher than it had dropped and played until I lost it from sight.

And my heart does not tell me that it will come back. For I believe it has another master.

* Music by Donato da Cascia (14th century).

Anonymous

(14th century)

[21] BALLAD (A.D. 1305) *Fuor de la bella bella caiba*

Out from the pretty, pretty cage the nightingale flies. The boy weeps when he finds his dear bird gone from the new cage, and sadly he says: "Who opened the door for it?" and sadly he says: "Who opened the door for it?"

He went to walk in a wood; he heard the little bird singing so sweetly. "O pretty bird, come back to my garden! O pretty bird, come back to my garden!"

[22] MARRIED WOMAN'S SONG *Non mi mandar messaggi, ché son falsi*

Send me no messengers, for they are false; send me no messengers, for they are evil.

Let your eyes be the messenger, when you raise them; let your eyes be the messenger to mine.

Look at my red lips, for I have a husband who does not know them.

[23] BALLAD *La mi tenne la staffa et io montai in arcione*

She held the stirrup for me, and I climbed into the saddle; she handed me the lance, and I put the shield on my arm; she gave me the sword and bound on the spur; she put on my helmet, and I talked to her of love.

"Good-bye, fair sister, for I am going to Avignon and from Avignon into France to win honor. If I strike a blow with my lance I will strike it for your love; if I die in battle I will die for your honor.

"The married women will say: 'Our lover is dead.' The maidens will say: 'He died for our love.' The widows will

say: 'It is right to do him honor. Where shall we bury him?
In St. Mary's of the Flower. With what shall we strew him?
With roses and violets.' "

[24] BALLATA: THE PILGRIM *I' son un pellegrin che vo cercando**

I am a pilgrim who goes seeking alms in God's name, begging for charity.

I go singing in my clear voice, with sweet looks and blonde hair. I own nothing but my staff and scrip.

I call and call, and no one answers. And when I think I am having fair sailing, a contrary wind comes raging down on me.

* Music by Giovanni da Cascia (fl. ca. 1340).

[25] BALLATA: LOVE SONG *Fior di dolcezza sei**

You are the flower of sweetness; my thoughts are of you only.

You only are my treasure, in whom are beauty and true modesty. For you I perish night and day, and my heart never stills from remembering you.

But if you do not grant me peace, my eyes will weep.

* Music by Francesco Landini (1325–1397).

[26] CACCIA: THE HUNT *Tosto che l'alba**

As soon as the dawn of the fair day appears, it wakes the hunters. "Get up, get up! it is time!" "Rouse the dogs!" "Hup, hup, Viola!" "Hup, Primera, hup!" "Up the mountain, with the good dogs in hand and the brachet hounds in the valley and everyone well posted on the slope!" "I see one of our best brachets breaking!" "Watch out!" "Draw the thickets on every side—Quaglina is giving tongue!" "Ho! ho! the hind is headed for you!" "Carbon has caught her, he is holding her with his teeth!"

The hunter on top of the mountain shouted: "To the next, to the next!" and sounded his horn.

* Music by Ghirardello da Firenze (14th century).

V·MOZARABIC

Refrains (Kharjas)

[1] *Tan te amaré, tan te amaré* (before A.D. 1042)

I will love you so much, I will love you so much, my lover,
I will love you so much! My sorrows have made my eyes
sick; oh, how they hurt!

[2] *Bokella al-'iqdi* (ca. 1100)

Mouth of pearls, sweet as honey, come and give me a kiss!
My lover, come to me.

[3] *Vais meu corazón de mib* (before 1140)

My heart leaves me; O my God, can it come back? My grief
for my lover is so great; he is sick, when will he be well?

[4] *Que faré mi mamma* (before 1149)

What shall I do, Mother? My lover is at the door!

[5] *Non quero, non, jillello* (12th century)

I will have no companion but my dark lover.

[6] *Que faré yo o que serad de mibi* (ca. 1250)

What shall I do or what will become of me? My lover, do
not leave me!

VI·SPANISH

Alfonso X

(1221 — 1284)

[1] IN PRAISE OF HOLY MARY, SHE BEING
BEAUTIFUL AND GOOD AND OF GREAT POWER
*Rosa das rosas e Fror das frores**

Rose of roses and flower of flowers, lady of ladies and sovereign of sovereigns!

Rose of beauty and semblance, flower of joy and pleasure, lady in being most merciful, sovereign in relieving grief and pain: *Rose of roses and flower of flowers, lady of ladies and sovereign of sovereigns!*

Such a liege lady a man should dearly love, for she can keep him from all evil and forgive him his sins which he commits in this world from evil desires: *Rose of roses and flower of flowers, lady of ladies and sovereign of sovereigns!*

Greatly must we love and serve her, for she ever strives to keep us from failing; she makes us repent of the wrongs that we commit as sinners: *Rose of roses and flower of flowers, lady of ladies and sovereign of sovereigns!*

This lady whom I make my liege and whose poet I seek to be—if in any way I can have her love, the devil take all other loves! *Rose of roses and flower of flowers, lady of ladies and sovereign of sovereigns!*

* From the *Cantigas de Santa Maria*, the language of which is Galician.

Anonymous

(13th century)

[2] CONCERNING LOVE *Qui triste tiene su coraçon*

If you are sad in heart, come listen. You will hear fine words, well rhymed, and all concerning love. He who rhymed them has gone to school and has always been devoted to ladies. He had his schooling in Germany and France and spent a long time in Lombardy learning the laws of courtesy.

One April day I had dined and was under an olive tree. High in an apple orchard I saw a silver cup; it was full of clear wine, red and of the best. It was covered so that the heat could not reach it. A lady had put it there, she who owned the orchard, so that when her lover came she could give him that wine to drink. Whoever should have such a wine at hand when he ate and should drink of it every day would never be sick again. High in the apple orchard too, I saw another cup. It was full of cold water from a spring in the orchard. I would gladly have drunk of it, only I feared it was enchanted.

I lay down with my head on the grass to avoid the noonday sun; I took off my clothes, fearing the heat. I found I was beside an ever-flowing fountain. No one ever saw its like. It had a great virtue: the chill that came from it was so great that if you walked around it you would not feel the heat. All sweet-smelling plants grew about that fountain: sage and roses and the lily and violets, and so many more that I cannot name them. But the fragrance that came from them would bring a dead man back to life.

I took a swallow of the water and was chilled all over. I took a flower in my hand—not the ugliest of them, you may be sure—and was going to sing of true love. But then I saw a damsel coming; never in my life had I seen a girl so beautiful. She was white and red, with short curls over her ears, she had a lovely white forehead, a face as fresh as an apple, a smooth, straight nose (you never saw one so well made), black, smiling eyes, a mouth to match, white teeth, red lips that were not too narrow but shaped to perfection. She was small around the waist, healthy, and well-proportioned. Her cloak and her dress were of no less than samite. She had a hat on her head to ward off the heat. On her hands were gloves that no serf gave her, you may be sure.

She came gathering flowers, singing in a high-pitched voice. Her song was of love and it ran: "Oh, my lover, shall I ever be with you! I love you today and will love you forever, as long as I live! That you are a scholar should make any woman love you the more. I never heard of any other man so accomplished. I would rather be with you than rule all Spain. But one thing troubles me: I fear that I am betrayed. For they say that another lady—courteous and beautiful and good—loves you passionately, she is mad for you. So I am afraid that you love her better. But if I can once see you, you will choose me to love, I know."

When my lady said this, she did not see me, you may be sure. But I know this: when she saw me she did not run away. I did not act like a churl; I rose and took her by the hand. Side by side we sat down under the olive tree. I said: "Tell me, my lady, have you ever known love?" She said: "I am deeply in love, but I do not know my lover. But a messenger from him has told me that he is a scholar and not a knight. He is well versed in making songs, he can read and sing. I am told that he comes of good blood, a youth with his first beard."

"In God's name tell me, my lady, what love gifts have you had from him?"

"These gloves and this hat, this coral and this ring—my lover sent me all these, and I wear them for love of him."

I recognized the fine things at once for I had sent them to her. She recognized my girdle at once for she had made it with her own hands. She took her cloak from her shoulders and kissed me on the mouth and the eyes. She had such joy in me that she could not even speak to me. She only said: "Lord God, I praise you that now I know my lover. All is well, now that I know my beloved."

When we had been there a long time recalling our love, she said: "My Lord, I must go back now, if you will let me."

I said: "Go, my lady, since you wish to go; but think of my love, by the faith that you owe me."

She said: "Be very sure of my love; I would not change you for an emperor."

My lady went quietly away, leaving me disconsolate. When I saw her, she was gone from the orchard. I nearly died. I wanted to go to sleep. But I saw a dove; it was as white as the snow of a mountain pass and it came flying through the orchard. . . . It had a gilded bell tied to its foot. I was going to the fountain, but when it saw me there, it went to the cup in the orchard. When it had entered the cup and had cooled itself, trying to come out quickly it spilled the water into the wine.

Pero González de Mendoza
(1340 — 1385)

[3] TO HIS LADY *Por Deus, senora, non me matedes**

In God's name, lady, do not kill me: you will gain nothing by my death.

In all truth and honor I have always loved you more than anything: if you kill me for loving you, what will you do to one who hates you?

I have always served you loyally, suffering great griefs and torment for you; you must not be so cruel, having me in your power.

When I am far from you, my longing for you begins to torment me; I die for you, O mirror of all perfections!

When you summoned me to speak with you, you promised never to deceive me. Keep your oath, lady, or you do me great wrong.

* Written in Galician.

Macias

(fl. 1360 — 1390)

[4] SONG *Pois me faleceu ventura**

Since fortune failed me in the time of delight, I expect no happiness, but to grieve forever. In torment and sadness I, too, will cry: *My God, my God, why hast thou forsaken me!*

Whoever hears of my woes and my sorrow and my fall and feels pity for me will join in this my complaint, and the more if he should know how great is my loss: *My God, my God, why hast thou forsaken me!*

* Written in Galician.

Diego Furtado de Mendoza

(died 1404)

[5] DANCE SONG *A aquel árbol, que mueve la foxa**

That tree there, moving its leaves: some longing has come upon it.

That tree there, beautiful to see, seems to want to put out flowers. *Some longing has come upon it.*

That tree there, beautiful to look at, seems to want to bloom. *Some longing has come upon it.*

Seems to want to put out flowers; they are showing already; go and see! *Some longing has come upon it.*

Seems to want to bloom; they are showing already; go and look! *Some longing has come upon it.*

They are showing already; go and see! Come, ladies, and pick the fruit. *Some longing has come upon it.*

* Written in Galician.

Alfonso Álvarez de Villasandino
(ca. 1350 — after 1423)

[6] IN PRAISE OF HIS LADY *Vysso enamoroso*

Face of love, have pity on me: I live in grief, desiring you. Your beauty put me in prison, for which misfortune sorrow never leaves my heart in any season, so does your countenance make me sad.

All my care is to praise you; I cannot forget that passed time. You would do right to think of me, for I have always served you loyally for no reward.

Every day I am sad and joyless. If but one day I could see you, your presence would comfort me; by it I should recover the good that I have lost.

[7] IN PRAISE OF DOÑA JUANA DE SOSA *De grant cuyta sofridor**

Burdened with great care I have been and am and shall always be, being the loyal lover of her whom I saw, see, and shall see. I have served, serve, and shall serve you, beautiful lady; in your love has been my hope and is and will be.

Though by great fear I have been tormented and am and shall be, thinking of your worth I have conquered and conquer and shall conquer. Therefore I have given and give and ever shall give great praise to God for that in such fashion I have spent and spend and shall spend my time.

Wherefore as long as I live I have said and say and shall say that to you I have turned and turn and shall turn this heart of mine. I have thought and think and shall think that, whether for good or for better, it is you, flower of flowers, whom I have loved and love and shall love.

Of your good name and your honor I have thought and think and shall think, wherefore great torment I have suffered and suffer and shall suffer. I have been and am and shall be constant—for my misfortune, alas!—to such a sorrow that I have lived in fear and so live and shall live.

* Written in Galician.

Álvaro de Luna

(1388 — 1453)

[8] SONG *Senyor Dios, pues me causaste*

Lord God, since you made me love beyond comparison, you must forgive me if I have broken your commandment.

You commanded that a man should love you before all things; and you caused this man to find a mistress so charming,

So generous, of fairer fame than all women whom you have created, Lord—she whom I love beyond comparison with a love that no mind can grasp.

You formed her in your image, Lord; you made me fall in love with your own pure holiness.

Your shaping such a shape as you shaped for her is reason enough for my sometimes forgetting you, who showed her to me.

Iñigo López de Mendoza,
Marqués de Santillana

(1398 — 1458)

[9] TO HIS LADY *El triste que se despide*

He who takes leave, leaves joy and pleasure, for his sad destiny makes him leave you, lovely being.

For him who asks such leave, feel grief, lady, for he asks it in despair, asking not life but certain death.

[10] TO HIS LADY *Si tu deseas a mi*

I do not know if you desire me; but I desire you, by my faith!

To no other have I given my faith; nor have I nor will I ever have another love. Happy the hour when first I saw you and spoke with you, for I gave myself to you wholly, *by my faith!*

I am yours in all truth; never doubt it, never think or dream otherwise. Since I have known you I am your captive, I have lost my heart and my mind, *by my faith!*

I love you and will love you always; always I will serve you. I have good reason, for I have chosen the best of ladies. I feign not nor have feigned, *by my faith!*

Juan de Mena
(1411 — 1456)

[11] SONG IN SICKNESS *Donde yago en esta cama*

As I lie here in bed my greatest pain is thinking of when I left my lady's arms.

In this sickness that is upon me, I repent of leaving you, I swear, as often as I think of you: so that those who know of it say that all the cause of my sickness is that *I left my lady's arms.*

Though I suffer and keep silent, my sad complaints are as near to me as your favors are far. If it is my end that now summons me, oh, what a death I lost by living on when *I left my lady's arms!*

Jorge Manrique

(1440 – 1479)

[12] TO HIS LADY *No se por que me fatigo*

I do not know why I struggle: I could not but be conquered, for I had no one on my side, and both you and I were against me.

You not loving me and I loving you, by your power and my consent we conquered me.

Since I was my enemy in yielding as I yielded, who will dare to befriend such an enemy of himself?

Altamira

(late 15th century)

[13] TO HIS LADY *Con dos cuydados guerreo*

I battle with two griefs which make me suffer and sigh: the one when I see you, the other when I do not see you.

Seeing you, I die for love and cannot help myself; not seeing you, I am in despair until I can see you again.

The one adds sigh to sigh, the other brings longing: I suffer when I see you, I die when I do not see you.

Gil Vicente

(ca. 1470 — ca. 1540)

[14] CHORAL SONG FROM A PLAY: TO THE
MOTHER OF THE DIVINE INFANT *Muy graciosa
es la doncella*

That girl is very winning; how lovely she is, how beautiful!

Tell me, you sailor who lives in ships, if ship or sail or star
is as beautiful.

Tell me, you knight who carries arms, if horse or arms or
war *is as beautiful.*

Tell me, you shepherd boy who tends the flock, if flock or
valley or mountain *is as beautiful.*

SOURCES

I · PROVENÇAL

WORKS CITED

Anglade, Joseph, *Anthologie des Troubadours,* Paris: E. de Boccard, n. d.

Appel, Carl, *Bernart von Ventadorn: Seine Lieder mit Einleitung und Glossar,* Halle: Max Niemeyer, 1915.

Appel, Carl, *Provenzalische Chrestomathie,* Leipzig: Reisland, 1907.

Archiv für das Studium der Neueren Sprachen und Literaturen, Braunschweig, 1846 ff.

Audiau, Jean, *La Pastourelle dans la poésie occitane du moyen-âge,* Paris: E. de Boccard, 1923.

Bartsch, Karl, *Chrestomathie provençale accompagnée d'une grammaire et d'un glossaire,* Ed. 4, Elberfeld: Friedrichs, 1880.

Cluzel, Irénée, "Trois 'unica' du troubadour catalan Cerveri (dit de Girona)," *Romania,* 77 (1956), pp. 66–77.

Kolsen, A., "25 bisher unedierte provenzalische Anonyma," *Zeitschrift für Romanische Philologie,* 38 (1914), pp. 281–310.

Kussler-Ratyé, Gabrielle, "Les chansons de la comtesse Béatrix de Dia," *Archivum Romanicum,* I (1917), pp. 161–82.

Le Roux de Lincy, A. J. V., *Recueil de chants historiques français depuis le XIIe jusqu'au XVIIIe siècle,* 2 vols., Paris, 1841.

Mahn, C. A. F., *Gedichte der Troubadours in provenzalischer Sprache,* 4 vols., Berlin, 1856–73.

Mahn, C. A. F., *Die Werke der Troubadours,* 4 vols., Berlin, 1846–54.

Massó y Torrents, J., "Riambau de Vaqueres en els cançoners catalans," Institut d'Estudis Catalans, *Anuari,* 1907, pp. 414–62.

Meyer, Paul, *Recueil d'anciens textes, bas-latins, provençaux et français,* Paris: Vieweg, 1877.

Milá y Fontanals, Manuel, *Poëtes lyriques catalans,* Paris, 1878.

Pillet, Alfred, and Henry Carstens, *Bibliographie der Troubadours,* Halle: Niemeyer, 1933.

Raynouard, F. J. M., *Choix des poésies originales des troubadours,* 6 vols., Paris, 1816–21.

Rochegude, *Le Parnasse occitanien, ou choix de poésies originales des troubadours,* Toulouse, 1819.

Schultz, Oscar, *Die Provenzalischen Dichterinnen: Biographien und Texte*, Leipzig, 1888.

Stimming, Albert, *Bertran de Born, sein Leben und seine Werke*, Halle, 1879.

Zeitschrift für Romanische Philologie, Halle, 1877 ff.

ORIGINAL TEXTS

Poem No.

1. Mahn, *Gedichte*, No. 297; Appel, *Chrestomathie*, p. 51.
2. Rochegude, *Parnasse*, p. 250; Appel, *Chrestomathie*, p. 53.
3. Raynouard, *Choix*, III, p. 101; Appel, *Chrestomathie*, p. 54.
4. Raynouard, *Choix*, III, p. 375; Appel, *Chrestomathie*, p. 96.
5. Raynouard, *Choix*, III, p. 86; Appel, *Bernart*, p. 195.
6. Raynouard, *Choix*, III, p. 44; Appel, *Bernart*, p. 188.
7. Mahn, *Werke*, I, p. 277; Stimming, *Bertran*, p. 226.
8. Schultz, *Dichterinnen*, p. 8; Kussler-Ratyé, "Chansons," p. 173.
9. Schultz, *Dichterinnen*, p. 18; Kussler-Ratyé, "Chansons," p. 164.
10. Meyer, *Recueil*, p. 82.
11. Massó y Torrents, "Riambau," p. 424.
12. Raynouard, *Choix*, III, p. 451; Appel, *Chrestomathie*, p. 84.
13. Raynouard, *Choix*, III, p. 82; Appel, *Chrestomathie*, p. 62.
14. Mahn, *Gedichte*, Nos. 547, 548, 549; Audiau, *La Pastourelle*, p. 34.
15. Mahn, *Werke*, III, p. 321; Schultz, *Dichterinnen*, p. 25.
16. Raynouard, *Choix*, V, p. 74; Appel, *Chrestomathie*, p. 91.
17. Mahn, *Werke*, III, p. 210.
18. Cluzel, "Trois 'unica,'" p. 69.
19. Mahn, *Werke*, IV, p. 75; Anglade, *Anthologie*, p. 176.
20. Bartsch, *Chrestomathie*, col. 227.
21. Mahn, *Gedichte*, I, p. 213.
22. *Zeitschrift*, 4, 509; Kolsen, "Anonyma," p. 296.
23. *Archiv*, 35, 109; Kolsen, "Anonyma," p. 294.
24. Le Roux de Lincy, *Chants historiques*, I, p. 79; Bartsch, *Chrestomathie*, col. 111.
25. Raynouard, *Choix*, II, p. 242; Bartsch, *Chrestomathie*, col. 245.
26. Appel, *Chrestomathie*, p. 85.

II · FRENCH

WORKS CITED

Bartsch, Karl, *Chrestomathie de l'ancien français (VIIIe-XVe siècles)*, 9th edition, Leipzig: F. C. W. Vogel, 1908.

Bartsch, Karl, *Romances et pastourelles françaises des XIIe et XIIIe siècles*, Leipzig: F. C. W. Vogel, 1870. (Abbreviated Bartsch, *R. & P.*)

Bédier, Joseph, and Jean Beck, *Les Chansons de Colin Muset*, Paris: Champion, 1912.

Brakelmann, Julius, "Die altfranzösische Liederhandschrift der Stadtbibliothek zu Bern," *Archiv für das Studium der Neueren Sprachen und Literaturen*, 41 (1867), pp. 339–376; 42 (1868), pp. 73–82, 241–392; 43 (1868), pp. 241–394.

Buchon, J. A., *Poésies de J. Froissart*, Paris, 1829.

Champion, Pierre, *Charles d'Orléans: Poésies*, 2 vols., Paris: Champion, 1923–1927.

Chichmaref, V., *Guillaume de Machaut: Poésies lyriques*, 2 vols., Paris: Champion, 1909.

Coussemaker, E. de, *Oeuvres complètes du trouvère Adam de la Halle*, Paris, 1872.

Gennrich, Friedrich, *Altfranzösische Lieder (1. Teil)*, Tübingen: Max Niemeyer Verlag, 1955.

Gennrich, Friedrich, *Rondeaux, Virelais und Balladen aus dem Ende des XII., dem XIII. und dem ersten Drittel des XIV. Jahrhunderts*, 3 vols., Dresden: Gesellschaft für Romanische Literatur, 1921–1963.

Jeanroy, Alfred, *Les Origines de la poésie lyrique en France au moyen âge*, 3rd ed., Paris: Champion, 1925.

Jeanroy, Alfred, *Oeuvres de François Villon avec une introduction et des notes*, Paris: Aux Éditions de la Chronique des Lettres Françaises, 1924.

Jubinal, A., *Nouveau recueil de contes, dits, fabliaux*, 2 vols., Paris, 1839–1842.

Meyer, P., "Des rapports de la poésie des trouvères avec celle des troubadours," *Romania*, 19 (1890), pp. 1–62.

Montaiglon, Anatole de, *Recueil général et complet des fabliaux des XIIIe et XIVe siècles*, Vol. I, Paris, 1872.

Nissen, Elisabeth, *Les chansons attribués à Guiot de Dijon et Jocelin*, Paris: Champion, 1928.

Paris, Gaston, *Chansons du XVe siècle*, Paris, 1875.

Paris, Gaston, "Les danseurs maudits," *Journal des Savants*, 1899, pp. 733–747.

Petersen Dyggve, Holger, *Gace Brulé, trouvère champenois, édition de chansons et étude historique*, Helsinki: Société Néophilologique de Helsinki, 1951.

Queux de Saint-Hilaire, Auguste, *Oeuvres complètes d'Eustache Deschamps*, 11 vols., Paris, 1878–1903.

Roy, Maurice, *Oeuvres poétiques de Christine de Pisan*, 3 vols., Paris, 1886–1896.

Steffens, G. "Der kritische Text der Gedichte von Richart de Semilli" in: *Beiträge zur romanischen und englischen Philol-*

ogie, Festgabe für Wendelin Foerster, Halle, 1902, pp. 331–362.

Stimming, Albert, *Die altfranzösischen Motette der Bamberger Handschrift nebst einem Anhang*, Dresden: Gesellschaft für Romanische Literatur, 1906.

Suchier, Hermann, *Oeuvres poétiques de Philippe de Remi, sire de Beaumanoir*, 2 vols., Paris, 1884–1885.

Wackernagel, Wilhelm, *Altfranzoesische Lieder und Leiche aus Handschriften zu Bern und Neuenberg*, Basel, 1846.

ORIGINAL TEXTS

Poem No.
1. Bartsch, *Chrestomathie*, p. 111.
2. *Ibid*, p. 160.
3. Petersen Dyggve, *Gace Brulé*, p. 428.
4. Steffens, "Kritische Text," p. 340.
5. Petersen Dyggve, *Gace Brulé*, p. 298.
6. Bartsch, *Chrestomathie*, p. 159.
7. Bartsch, *R. & P.*, p. 76.
8. Nissen, *Guiot*, p. 1.
9. Bédier & Beck, *Colin Muset*, p. 27.
10. Brakelmann, "Liederhandschrift," 43, p. 293.
11. Jeanroy, *Origines*, p. 501.
12. Coussemaker, *Adam*, p. 232.
13. Suchier, *Philippe de Remi*, II, p. 306.
14. *Ibid.*, p. 305.
15. Chichmaref, *Machaut*, II, p. 556.
16. *Ibid.*, p. 572.
17. Buchon, *Froissart*, p. 464.
18. Queux de Saint-Hilaire, *Deschamps*, IV, p. 9.
19. Roy, *Christine de Pisan*, I, p. 5.
20. Champion, *Charles d'Orléans*, I, p. 235.
21. *Ibid.*, p. 246.
22. *Ibid.*
23. *Ibid.*, p. 256.
24. Jeanroy, *Villon*, p. 51.
25. Bartsch, *Chrestomathie*, p. 107.
26. Jeanroy, *Origines*, p. 498.
27. Wackernagel, *Altfranzoesische Lieder*, p. 12.
28. Jeanroy, *Origines*, p. 499.
29. Bartsch, *R. & P.*, p. 27.
30. Bartsch, *R. & P.*, p. 20; Gennrich, *Altfranzösische Lieder*, p. 54.
31. Bartsch, *R. & P.*, p. 20; Gennrich, *Altfranzösische Lieder*, p. 55.
32. Gennrich, *Rondeaux, Virelais und Balladen*, I, No. 95.

33. Stimming, *Altfranzösischen Motette*, p. 14.
34. *Ibid.*, p. 39.
35. Bartsch, *R. & P.*, p. 23.
36. Meyer, "Rapports," p. 57.
37. Paris, *Chansons*, p. 30.
38. *Ibid.*, p. 63.
39. *Ibid.*, p. 145.
40. *Ibid.*, p. 36.
41. *Ibid.*, p. 29.
42. Jubinal, *Nouveau recueil*, II, p. 214.
43. Paris, "Les danseurs maudits," p. 744.
44. Bartsch, *R. & P.*, p. 18.
45. I–XX: Bartsch, *R. & P.*, pp. 8, 14, 17, 28, 36, 38, 40, 87, 105, 112, 117, 127, 145, 169, 177, 196, 209, 211, 270, 284.
   XXI: Montaiglon, *Recueil général*, I, p. 141.
   XXII: Stimming, *Altfranzösischen Motette*, p. 171.

III · GERMAN

WORKS CITED

Bartsch, Karl, *Deutsche Liederdichter des zwölften bis vierzehnten Jahrhunderts*, 8th edition (ed. W. Golter), Berlin: B. Behr's Verlag, 1928.

Des Minnesangs Frühling, 33rd edition (ed. Carl von Kraus), Stuttgart: S. Hirzel Verlag, 1962.

Güntter, Otto, *Walther von der Vogelweide mit einer Auswahl aus Minnesang und Spruchdichtung*, Leipzig: G. J. Goschen'sche Verlag, 1899.

Jantzen, Hermann, *Literaturdenkmäler des 14. und 15. Jahrhunderts*, Berlin and Leipzig: Walter de Gruyter & Co., 1919.

Kuhn, Hugo, *Minnesang des 13. Jahrhunderts: Aus Carl von Kraus' "Deutschen Liederdichtern" ausgewählt*, 2nd edition, Tübingen: Max Niemeyer Verlag, 1962.

Pfeiffer, Franz, and Karl Bartsch, *Walther von der Vogelweide*, 7th edition (ed. H. Michel), Leipzig: F. A. Brockhaus, 1911.

ORIGINAL TEXTS

Poem No.
1. *Des Minnesangs Frühling*, p. 5.
2. *Ibid.*
3. *Ibid.*, p. 33.
4. *Ibid.*, p. 32.
5. *Ibid.*, p. 8.
6. Bartsch, *Liederdichter*, p. 28.

7. *Des Minnesangs Frühling*, p. 43.
8. *Ibid.*, p. 87.
9. *Ibid.*, p. 120.
10. *Des Minnesangs Frühling*, p. 228; Bartsch, *Liederdichter*, p. 68.
11. *Des Minnesangs Frühling*, p. 189; Bartsch, *Liederdichter*, p. 59.
12. *Des Minnesangs Frühling*, p. 180.
13. Pfeiffer and Bartsch, *Walther*, p. 16.
14. *Ibid.*, p. 209.
15. Kuhn, *Minnesang*, p. 48.
16. Bartsch, *Liederdichter*, p. 150.
17. Kuhn, *Minnesang*, p. 26.
18. *Ibid.*, p. 29.
19. Kuhn, *Minnesang*, p. 28; Bartsch, *Liederdichter*, p. 204.
20. Bartsch, *Liederdichter*, p. 228.
21. Güntter, *Walther*, p. 116.
22. Kuhn, *Minnesang*, p. 2.
23. Bartsch, *Liederdichter*, p. 303.
24. *Ibid.*, p. 325.
25. *Ibid.*, p. 338.
26. *Des Minnesangs Frühling*, p. 1.
27. *Ibid.*
28. *Ibid.*, p. 2.
29. Bartsch, *Liederdichter*, p. 368.
30. Jantzen, *Literaturdenkmäler*, p. 47.

IV · ITALIAN

WORKS CITED

Carducci, Giosuè, *Cantilene e ballate, strambotti e madrigali nei secoli XIII e XIV*, Sesto S. Giovanni: Madella, 1914.

Contini, Gianfranco, *Poeti del duecento*, 2 vols., Milan: Ricciardi, 1960.

Dante Alighieri, *Rime* (ed. Gianfranco Contini), Turin: Einaudi, 1946.

Di Benedetto, Luigi, *Rimatori del dolce stil novo*, Turin: Unione Tipografico-Editrice Torinese, 1925.

Egidi, Francesco, *Le Rime di Guittone d'Arezzo*, Bari: Laterza, 1940.

Levi, Eugenia, *Lirica italiana antica: novissima scelta di rime dei secoli XIII, XIIII, XV*, Florence: Olschki, 1905.

Monaci, Ernesto, *Crestomazia italiana dei primi secoli*, new ed., Rome: Società Editrice Dante Alighieri, 1955.

Panvini, Bruno, *La Scuola poetica siciliana: Le canzoni dei rimatori nativi di Sicilia,* Florence: Olschki, 1955. (Abbreviated Panvini, *Siciliani.*)

Panvini, Bruno, *La Scuola poetica siciliana: Le canzoni dei rimatori non siciliani,* 2 vols., Florence: Olschki, 1957–1958. (Abbreviated Panvini, *Non Siciliani.*)

Sapegno, Natalino, *Poeti minori del trecento,* Milan: Ricciardi, 1952.

Sapegno, Natalino, *Scrittori d'Italia,* Volume I: *Secoli XIII–XV,* 3rd ed., Florence: La Nuova Italia, 1945.

Vitale, Maurizio, *Rimatori comici-realistici del due e trecento,* 2 vols., Turin: Unione Tipografico-Editrice Torinese, 1956.

ORIGINAL TEXTS

Poem No.

1. Sapegno, *Scrittori,* I, p. 8; Monaci, *Crestomazia,* p. 54.
2. Monaci, *Crestomazia,* p. 74; Panvini, *Siciliani,* p. 87.
3. Sapegno, *Scrittori,* I, p. 27; Panvini, *Non Siciliani,* I, p. 62.
4. Monaci, *Crestomazia,* p. 106; Panvini, *Siciliani,* p. 139.
5. Monaci, *Crestomazia,* p. 107; Sapegno, *Scrittori,* I, p. 42.
6. Monaci, *Crestomazia,* p. 117; Panvini, *Non Siciliani,* I, p. 49.
7. Monaci, *Crestomazia,* p. 125; Sapegno, *Scrittori,* I, p. 36.
8. Contini, *Poeti del duecento,* I, p. 165.
9. Carducci, *Cantilene,* p. 7; Monaci, *Crestomazia,* p. 129.
10. Monaci, *Crestomazia,* p. 260; Panvini, *Siciliani,* p. 110.
11. Monaci, *Crestomazia,* p. 222; Egidi, *Rime di Guittone,* p. 107.
12. Contini, *Poeti del duecento,* II, p. 73.
13. Monaci, *Crestomazia,* p. 289.
14. *Ibid.,* p. 326.
15. Vitale, *Rimatori comici-realistici,* I, p. 298.
16. Sapegno, *Scrittori,* I, p. 66; Di Benedetto, *Rimatori,* p. 60.
17. Vitale, *Rimatori comici-realistici,* II, p. 98.
18. Dante Alighieri, *Rime* (ed. Contini), p. 155.
19. Vitale, *Rimatori comici-realistici,* II, p. 300.
20. Sapegno, *Poeti minori,* p. 471; Carducci, *Cantilene,* p. 283.
21. Carducci, *Cantilene,* p. 53.
22. *Ibid.,* p. 65.
23. Levi, *Lirica italiana antica,* p. 149.
24. Sapegno, *Poeti minori,* p. 509.
25. *Ibid.,* p. 498.
26. *Ibid.,* p. 524.

V · MOZARABIC

WORKS CITED

García Gómez, E., "Veinticuatro jaryas romances en muwaš-šaḥas árabes," *Al-Andalus*, 1952, pp. 57–127.
Stern, S. M., "Les vers finaux en espagnol dans les muwaššaḥs hispano-hébraïques," *Al-Andalus*, 1948, pp. 299–346.
Stern, S. M., *Les Chansons mozarabes*, Palermo: U. Manfredi, 1953.

ORIGINAL TEXTS

Poem No.
1. Stern, "Vers finaux," No. 18.
2. Stern, *Chansons mozarabes*, No. 47.
3. Stern, "Vers finaux," No. 9.
4. *Ibid.*, No. 14.
5. García Gómez, "Veinticuatro jaryas," No. XIII.
6. Stern, "Vers finaux," No. 16.

VI · SPANISH

WORKS CITED

Alfonso X, [Afonso X, o Sábio], *Cantigas de Santa Maria* (ed. W. Mettman), Vol. I, Coimbra: [University of Coimbra], 1959.
Amador de los Ríos, José, *Historia crítica de la literatura española*, 7 vols., Madrid, 1861–1865.
Foulché-Delbosc, R., *Cancionero castellano del siglo XV*, 2 vols., Madrid: Bailly-Baillère, 1912–1915.
Lang, Henry R., *Cancioneiro gallego-castelhano*, New Haven: Yale University Press, 1913.
Menéndez Pidal, Ramón, "Razon de Amor, con los Denuestos del Agua y del Vino," *Revue Hispanique*, 13 (1905), pp. 602–618.
Ochoa, Eugenio de, and P. J. Pidal, *El Cancionero de Juan Alfonso de Baena (siglo XV)*, Madrid, 1851. (Abbreviated Ochoa, *CB*.)
Santillana, Marqués de, *Canciones e decires* (ed. V. Garcia de Diego), Madrid: "La Lectura," 1913.

Vicente, Gil, *Obras* (ed. J. V. Barreto Feio and J. G. Monteiro), 3 vols, Hamburg, 1834.

ORIGINAL TEXTS

Poem No.
 1. Alfonso X, *Cantigas*, I, p. 33.
 2. Menéndez Pidal, "Razon de Amor," pp. 602 ff.
 3. Ochoa, *CB*, p. 257.
 4. Lang, *Cancioneiro gallego-castelhano*, p. 12.
 5. Amador de los Ríos, *Historia crítica*, V, p. 293.
 6. Ochoa, *CB*, p. 49.
 7. *Ibid.*, p. 50.
 8. *Ibid.*, p. 1.
 9. Santillana, *Canciones y decires*, p. 255.
10. *Ibid.*, p. 233.
11. Foulché-Delbosc, *Cancionero castellano del siglo XV*, I, p. 215.
12. *Ibid.*, II, p. 488.
13. *Ibid.*, II, p. 760.
14. Vicente, *Obras*, I, p. 61.

APPENDIX:

SELECTED DISCOGRAPHY

DISCS AND ALBUMS CITED

AL 14, AL 72 (Allegro): *Music of the Gothic Period and the Early Renaissance*, Vol. I, Vol. II.

ARC 3002 (Archive Production): Adam de la Halle, *13 Rondeaux*.

    ARC 3003: *Madrigale e Caccie from the Codex of Antonio Squarcialupi*.

    ARC 3032: Guillaume de Machaut, *La Messe de Notre Dame* and *10 Secular Works*.

    ARC 3051: *Chansons et Motets du 13ᵉ siècle*.

CND 9 (Club National du Disque): *La Musique et la Poésie Française*.

EA 0012 (Expériences Anonymes): *Troubadour and Trouvère Songs (XII & XIII Centuries)*.

    EA 0023: *Las Cantigas de Santa Maria del Rey Alfonso El Sabio*.

EMS 201 (E.M.S. Recordings): *Music of the Twelfth and Thirteenth Centuries*.

LL 85 (Lyrichord): *Music of the Middle Ages*.

LM 6015, LM 6016 (RCA Victor): *History of Music in Sound*, Vol. II, Vol. III.

LM 40000(10) (RCA Victor Italiana): *Storia della Musica Italiana (History of Italian Music)*, Vol. I.

XWN 18166 (Westminster): Guillaume de Machaut, *Motets, Ballades, Virelais, and Rondeaux*.

    XWN 18683: *French Troubadour Songs*.

    XWN 18848: *German Songs of the Middle Ages and the Renaissance*.

INDIVIDUAL RECORDINGS

Provençal

Anonymous, "A l'entrada del tems clar": ARC 3002, Columbia (England) DF 102 (78 rpm).

Bernart de Ventadorn. Other songs of his: ARC 3051, EA 0012, EMS 201, LL 85, LM 6015.

Giraut de Bornelh, "Reis glorios": EA 0012.

Guiraut Riquier. Other songs of his: ARC 3051, EA 0012.

Jaufre Rudel, "Lanquan li jorn": ARC 3051.
Raimbaut de Vaqueiras. Other songs of his: AL 14, LL 85.

French

Anonymous, "Por coi me bat mes maris": XWN 18166 (as third voice of a motet).
Anonymous, "Volez vos que je vos chant": ARC 3051.
Adam de la Halle, "Tant con je vivrai": LM 6016. Other songs of his: ARC 3002.
Chastelain de Coucy. Another song of his: Victor 20227 (78 rpm).
Colin Muset, "Quant je voy yver retorner": LM 6015 (as "anonymous").
Froissart. Another song of his: CND 9.
Gace Brulé, "Cil qui d'amours me conseille": EA 0012.
Guiot de Dijon, "Chanterai por mon corage": LM 6015.
Machaut, "De toutes flours" and "Rose, lis, printemps": XWN 18166. Other songs of his, together with his "Notre Dame Mass": ARC 3032.

German

Friedrich von Hausen. Another song of his: Decca 38180–81 (78 rpm).
Neidhart. Other songs of his: EMS 201, LL 85.
Walther von der Vogelweide. Other songs of his: LL 85, XWN 18848.

Italian

Anonymous, "I' son un pellegrin": AL 72, LM 40000(10).
Anonymous, "Tosto che l'alba": ARC 3003, LM 40000(10).
Other songs set by the same school of composers (whom some scholars believe to have composed the words as well) also in ARC 3003 and LM 40000(10).

Spanish

Alfonso X. Other songs of his: EA 0023, LM 6015.

INDEX OF ORIGINAL FIRST LINES*

French

Ahi! Amours, con dure departie, 58

Chanterai por mon corage, 61
Cil qui d'amours me conseille, 57
Coment que longe demore, 54
Crevez moy les yeulx, 71
Cuers qui dort, il n'aimme pas, 78

Dame des cieulx, regente terrienne, 73
D'amors qui m'a tolu a moi, 52
De toutes flours n'avoit et de tous fruis, 66

En dist camors est douce chose, 75
Entre moi et mon amin, 76

Gentil duc de Lorraine, prince de grant renom, 80

He! Dieux, quel dueil, quel rage, quel meschief, 70
Hellas! il est fait de ma vie, 81

J'aim la plus sade riens qui soit de mere nee, 55
Ja nus hons pris ne dira sa reson, 53
J'ay bien nourry sept ans ung joly gay, 81
J'ay veu la beauté m'amye, 80
Je chantasse par revel, 78
Jherusalem, grant damage me fais, 75

L'amour de moy sy est enclose, 80
Lasse, pour quoi refusai, 76
L'autrier avint en cel autre pais, 59
Le voulez vous, 71
Li pes d'un sueron, 65
Li solex luist et clers et biaux, 74
Li sons d'un cornet, 82

Mon seul amy, mon bien, ma joye, 71
(Myn hert hath send Glad Hope in hys message, 72)

* Since they do not begin the poems in which they occur, the Mozarabic *kharjas* and French *refrains* are not included in this index.
References are to pages.

German

Italian

Spanish

A aquel árbol que mueve la foxa, 135

Con dos cuydados guerreo, 141

De grant cuyta sofridor, 136
Donde yago en esta cama, 140

El triste que se despide, 139

Muy graciosa es la doncella, 142

No se por que me fatigo, 141

Pois me faleceu ventura, 135
Por Deus, senora, non me matedes, 134

Qui triste tiene su coraçon, 131

Rosa das rosas e Fror das frores, 130

Senyor Dios, pues me causaste, 138
Si tu deseas a mi, 139

Vysso enamoroso, 136

INDEX OF POETS*

* References are to pages.

ABOUT THE COMPILER AND TRANSLATOR

Willard R. Trask spent his childhood in Germany, Russia, France, England, and Panama. He was educated in New England and France, eventually specializing in medieval literature. Eminent as a scholar, author, and translator, he has published a biography, *Joan of Arc: Self Portrait*, and some thirty translations of both literary and scholarly works from French, German, Portuguese, and Spanish. His translation of the first volume of Casanova's *History of My Life* was awarded the 1967 National Book Award for translation. In addition, Mr. Trask has received several Bollingen Foundation grants for his work in medieval and primitive poetry, and has twice held the E. A. Robinson Fellowship of the Edward MacDowell Association. Most recently Mr. Trask has been lecturer in the Humanities at Juniata College, Huntingdon, Pennsylvania, where he has given courses on the medieval European lyric and on translations.